Text copyright © 2018 by Career Tree Network
All rights reserved.

No part of this book may be reproduced, or stored in a retrieval system, or transmitted in any form or by any means, electronic, mechanical, photocopying, recording, or otherwise, without express written permission of Career Tree Network.

Career Tree Network
6650 W. State Street Unit D
Milwaukee, Wisconsin 53213

For general inquires, please contact: info@careertreenetwork.com

ISBN-13: 978-1979412513
ISBN-10: 1979412510

Printed in the United States of America

200 WORDS

Essential Career Advice
for Therapy Professionals

Career Tree Network

INTRODUCTION

Congratulations on your decision to become a therapy professional! In this book, you will find advice and perspectives from experienced professionals who want to see people like you succeed and flourish in the field. A group of professionals, including recent graduates, professors, rehab managers, private practice owners, hiring managers, employers, human resources directors, recruiters, professional association members, and travel therapists all contributed to the creation of this book. They offer insights on graduating school, finding jobs, finding residency programs, career advancement, exploring new career paths, opening a private practice, and everything in between. Welcome to 200 Words, a rich compilation of career advice for therapy professionals!

Career Tree Network

TABLE OF CONTENTS

- **09** Advice and Perspectives From Recent Graduates
- **17** Searching for a Job
- **35** Resumes, Cover Letters, References, & Applications
- **71** Interviews
- **101** Residency Programs
- **109** Working with Recruiters
- **117** Salary Conversations
- **129** Starting & Working in a New Job
- **145** Networking and Professional Development
- **169** Job Relocation
- **175** Exploring Jobs Outside of Your Ideal Practice Setting
- **179** Advice and Perspectives from Therapy Professionals Who Work in Academics
- **189** Travel Positions
- **203** Mentors & Mentees
- **209** Promotions
- **215** Advice and Perspectives from Therapists in Leadership Positions
- **231** Leaving your Current Job
- **237** Advice and Perspectives from Private Practice Owners
- **247** The Business Side of Healthcare and Therapy
- **255** The Future of Physical Therapy

200 WORDS

ADVICE AND PERSPECTIVES FROM RECENT GRADUATES

ESSENTIAL CAREER ADVICE FOR THERAPY PROFESSIONALS

WHAT ADVICE DO YOU HAVE FOR A GRADUATING STUDENT IN SEARCH OF THEIR FIRST POSITION?

Do not be afraid of starting a position in an area that isn't your first choice. Consider putting a higher priority on the environment of care that you observe throughout the interview process rather than a particular practice setting.

If you feel like the staff and leadership are good fits for you, then the actual patient care setting will inevitably be a good fit for you too.

WHAT ADVICE DO YOU HAVE FOR SOMEONE WITHIN THE LAST YEAR OF SCHOOL?

In your last year of school, it is important to work diligently on having exceptional relationships with your clinical instructors. Ensure that your time spent in clinical internships is as beneficial as possible to your development as a therapist.

Remember that your instructors are incredible resources to be listed as references and can open doors to opportunities down the road. You want to genuinely invest in what is being taught and prioritize that relationship.

WHAT ADVICE DO YOU HAVE FOR A GRADUATING STUDENT IN SEARCH OF THEIR FIRST POSITION OR SOMEONE EARLY IN THEIR CAREER?

For your first position, look to diversify and build a solid foundation for your career. At the same time, try to find a specific area of interest in which you can dig deep and acquire exceptional skills and knowledge. Become an expert within a niche. Remember that it's not about you, it's about your patients. Look for a position that allows you to express yourself through your work.

Ask about the clinical growth opportunities within a company. For example, some companies offer mentoring programs for new grads and practitioners that are new to a different practice. This provides support and guidance as well as a likelihood of work satisfaction and retention during those initial months in the field. Many companies advertise their special skill set and having those resources to support that growth of their clinicians again offers an environment of life long learning that many therapists appreciate.

Don't get sucked in to a position that doesn't have a good support system in place. You don't want to end up on an island early in your career. You should look for a positive working environment. Follow your intuition and trust that feeling.

WHAT DO YOU WISH YOU WOULD HAVE KNOWN ABOUT THE JOB SEARCH PROCESS WHILE YOU WERE STILL IN SCHOOL?

While you are still in school, start to network within your professional association. The more networked you are at the time of graduation, the easier it is to be introduced to different job opportunities.

Contrary to what many therapists believe, it's far less likely that you'll find a job on Indeed or similar sites, and more likely that you will be introduced to an opportunity by someone within your network.

It's very important to be present and involved within your professional association as early as possible.

WHAT IS SOMETHING THAT MOST STUDENTS PROBABLY DON'T REALIZE ABOUT WORKING AS A THERAPY PROFESSIONAL?

As a student, it's very common to be focused on the didactic program of your learning, such as lectures and coursework. But when you actually begin to work in your field, you'll find that the majority of knowledge and information that you will use throughout your career is probably what you learn by working with your patients along the way.

EXPERIENCE IS THE BEST TEACHER!

200 WORDS

SEARCHING
FOR A JOB

ESSENTIAL CAREER ADVICE FOR THERAPY PROFESSIONALS

HOW DO I KNOW WHEN IT'S TIME TO LEAVE MY CURRENT POSITION AND PURSUE A NEW OPPORTUNITY?

YOU SHOULD FEEL GOOD WHEN YOU WALK INTO WORK.

If you're not answering yes to these questions on most days, it's time to look for something else.

- Do I enjoy what I'm doing? Am I relatively happy going to work? When I walk into work, am I relatively happy with the whole picture? When I first set foot in the office, what's my overall disposition?
- Do I feel like I'm making a difference in the lives of my patients? Does the work that I'm doing matter? Is it making an impact?

You should feel good when you go into work. From a therapy perspective, it's important to feel like you're making an impact.

OK, I'M READY FOR A NEW POSITION. HOW CAN I JUMP START MY CAREER SEARCH?

It's great that you're ready to take the plunge! Here are four simple tasks to formally kick off your search.

1. REACH OUT TO YOUR NETWORK.
As you begin your search it's time to reach out to your professional network to let them know about your search and to ask for their assistance. Craft an email to a select group of trusted colleagues.

2. UPDATE YOUR RESUME
Do a revamp of your resume. Include your most recent job responsibilities as well as new industry buzz words or recent professional certifications that you've accomplished.

3. BURN SOME BRIDGES.
Turn down that promotion at your currently employer. Consider telling your boss that you're looking for employment elsewhere. The key here is to draw a line in the sand so that you commit to the job search and the opportunity for employment elsewhere.

4. FOCUS YOUR EFFORTS ON THREE OPPORTUNITIES AT A TIME.
You can't be all things to all people. It's important that you stay focused during the job search process. Remember if you chase two rabbits, both will escape. Set your priorities and opportunities and then strategically pursue those positions most in line with your career goals.

Career Tree Network

WHAT SHOULD I KNOW ABOUT THE HIRING PROCESS?

The hiring process takes longer than most people think it should.

It's been said in the HR world "hire slowly and fire quickly." When applying for jobs, people tend to get frustrated because of delays or a lack of communication. Remember that things do typically go slower than you'd like, but that doesn't mean they're not moving along.

One thing that many prospective employees forget is to take their time and ensure that there is a good mutual fit. The hiring process is a two-way street. While the employer is evaluating you, you should also be evaluating the employer. It's less than ideal to start a position only to leave after a few months.

As an employee, you should be happy in your position. Too often, candidates accept the first position they're offered and forget to ask whether that position meets their needs.

Remember this: you may have to apply for more jobs than you want to in order to find the right fit. You don't have to accept the first offer that comes your way. There is an employer out there that will match your needs!

WHAT STEPS DOES AN EMPLOYER FOLLOW WITHIN A TYPICAL HIRING PROCESS?

Once a candidate has applied for a position, a Human Resources representative will go through and screen the applicant. Within the screening process, they will look at your resume and additional application materials in order to evaluate a potential fit for the position.

Once the screening process is complete, if they've decided that they want to talk to you, they will typically schedule a phone interview. Phone interviews act as an additional screening tool to learn more about you and fill in any details that may be unclear.

The next step is the in-person interview. Typically, in-person interviews are with the hiring manager. The hiring manager is the one who will ultimately make the final hiring decision, while the HR representative's job is to provide them with suitable candidates.

What happens after an in-person interview can vary from employer to employer. There may be a second in-person interview, or they may go directly into the rejection/offer process.

HOW LONG CAN I EXPECT THE HIRING PROCESS TO TAKE?

From the time you submit your resume to the time you receive an offer or rejection, it could be two days or two months. In a perfect world, the employer would get back to you within a week. However, the timeline primarily depends on how eager the employer is to fill the opening. If the need is urgent, the process will move quickly. If it's not a time-sensitive matter, you can expect that the hiring process will drag out longer as the employer likely has other priorities.

WHAT SKILLS DO EMPLOYERS LOOK FOR IN A THERAPY PROFESSIONAL?

First and foremost, employers want to see that you are confident in your clinical skills. Whether you're a new grad or a therapist of 30 years, having a solid foundation and belief in your skills is very important.

Confidence grows over time, but even new grads can trust the education and training that they've received. Employers won't believe you can impact patient lives if you don't believe it first!

Aside from clinical skills, employers want to see that you are professional, have good communication skills, and can understand the business side of therapy. Whatever job you take, it entails more than just showing up and treating patients. You also have to have a knowledge of how the clinic runs and the economic engine of the industry.

WHAT DO YOU LOOK FOR WHEN HIRING A THERAPY PROFESSIONAL?

When hiring therapists, employers look for clinical expertise. They want to see that you're experienced and knowledgeable in your particular setting and patient population. They also look for a strong clinical focus and diverse clinical background.

Hiring managers value flexibility and adaptability. When working in close quarters, it's important to have therapists on staff who are able to coexist and cooperate with one another.

IF THE POSITION I WANT ISN'T CURRENTLY OPEN, HOW SHOULD I PURSUE IT?

Networking is extremely important in the job search process. Once you've identified an organization that you want to work for, it's in your best interest to make as many connections as possible.

Often, positions are filled organically through employee connections before ever being posted anywhere online.

When you find an employer that is a good fit but doesn't currently have any openings, you may want to stop by a clinic or call them to make your interest known. You could find them on LinkedIn or other social media sites and introduce yourself as a professional colleague with interest in their organization. That way, when positions open up, your name is more likely to come to mind.

Ultimately, you want to build relationships within the organization. Name your interest and availability and ask that they would keep you in mind when a position becomes available.

It's also a good idea to follow up every three to six months to reaffirm your interest and ask if there are any new openings.

Career Tree Network

WHAT DOES A PRIVATE PRACTICE OWNER LOOK FOR WHEN HIRING A THERAPY PROFESSIONAL?

First and foremost, private practice owners look to see that you have experience in what the clinic does. It's not necessary to have experience in every little niche thing that a clinic offers, but it's important to have at least some experience.

Good referrals, a steady work history, and eagerness to learn, are also important to the hiring process. Each clinic is different than the next, so therapists who can adapt to unique populations and practices are valuable.

Private practice owners also look for therapists who have good bedside manners, can relate well to patients, and are eager and energetic throughout the hiring process.

Owners are impressed by therapists who truly desire to learn and grow in order to become the best clinicians they can. Character comes before everything else.

HOW CAN I TELL IF A JOB OFFER IS RIGHT FOR ME OR IF I SHOULD KEEP LOOKING?

Only you know what the right position is. When starting your job search, you should have a list of non-negotiables. Maybe you're unwilling to work more than 30 minutes away, or you need your employer to offer health insurance.

Whatever your must-have attributes are, you should try to only look at openings that offer those perks. However, while there might be two or three things you absolutely can't budge on, there are likely many more that you'd like, but don't necessarily need.

You won't always get everything you want, so it's important to distinguish what is most important to you. Once you've made it through the interview process and an offer is extended, you've likely had enough interaction with the staff and facility that you're able to judge whether, based on the culture and your requirements, the position would be a good fit.

Career Tree Network

HOW DO I PRIORITIZE WHAT IS MOST IMPORTANT WHEN LOOKING FOR THE PERFECT POSITION?

When you're looking for a new position, whether you've just graduated or you're making the switch from a current job, you should be able to identify what it is you're hoping to get out of the job. Look at your career goals and ask what types of positions will help you achieve those milestones.

After you've identified your potential employers based on geographic location and practice setting, you can start to dive into other benefits and drawbacks of the organizations.

It can seem overwhelming when you begin the job search, but if you narrow down what's most important to you and your career, you'll probably find that there are many resources available to help you in your job search.

WHAT ATTRIBUTES SHOULD I LOOK FOR IN A WORK ENVIRONMENT?

Work environment is important. The ideal workplace is different for every therapist, based on their values and experiences.

In order to put a name to your ideal work environment, ask yourself what's the most exciting part of going in to work each day.

Is it your coworkers? Look for a workplace that values teamwork and emphasizes collaborative work among therapists.

Is it the leadership? Take your time to scope out the management. Do some research to learn what the leadership style is and make sure it's something you respect and feel comfortable with.

While no workplace is perfect, and you'll likely have to compromise on some of your checklist items, it's okay to have some non-negotiable attributes in your job search.

HOW DO I DEFINE MY DREAM POSITION?

If you don't know what you want, it will be hard to find it. The first step is to build a clear definition of your dream career opportunity. Your dream can be defined by a few different criteria:

1. **Location** – In what geographic location would you like to work?
2. **Company** – What companies would you really like to work for?
3. **Job Title** – Do you have a certain job title that you'd like to have?
4. **Job Type** – Would you like to work part-time or full-time?

Based on your answers to the criteria above, you should build an Objective Statement. This Objective Statement can also fit nicely at the top of your resume. Your statement should answer the four criteria above. Here is an example: "I'm looking for a full-time Pediatric Physical Therapist position in Green Bay."

With your objective statement in hand, you can now develop a list of 5-10 organizations that have the type of position that you're looking for. You don't need to check their current employment openings, rather just create a master list of organizations that could potentially fit your dream criteria.

HOW DO I NARROW DOWN THE EMPLOYERS I WANT TO PURSUE?

Most therapy professionals narrow down employers based on geographic location and practice setting. Are you open to relocate? If so, your potential employers expand greatly. If not, depending on the size of the geographic location where you currently live or want to live, there are only a certain number of employers within reasonable driving distance from your home.

Within the organizations that are geographically convenient, there will likely be an ideal practice setting. For example, you can weed out Home Health and Outpatient clinics if you're only open to Skilled Nursing.

If you're still having trouble narrowing it down, the internet can be a wonderful resource. Look at reviews of employers by current and past employees and scan their social media accounts. You can also use your professional network of professors, classmates, and coworkers to see if a certain employer has a reputation.

One of the best ways to identify whether an employer would be worth pursuing is by going in and directly visiting the facility to see what the culture is like. You can talk to employees and get a feel for whether the organization is a good match for you.

HOW LONG IS THE TYPICAL JOB SEARCH PROCESS FROM EMPLOYMENT APPLICATION TO JOB OFFER?

The process itself can vary in length depending on the urgency that the employer feels to fill the opening. Within any hiring process, there may be a delay anywhere from a few hours to a few weeks.

After the employer reviews your application, you should hear from them within a few days regardless of the outcome.

The typical hiring process from start to finish includes the application, phone interview, in-person interview, reference check, background check, and offer.

The quickest the entire process could take is about five days, but it could last up to four weeks from start to finish.

Most employers try to move quickly through the hiring process because the best candidates are typically only available for a short period of time.

As a candidate, you can tell a lot about an organization based on their hiring process. Do they respect you and move quickly? If they recognize your skills and value, the answer will be yes. If they delay, however, it might not be the best fit.

200 WORDS

RESUMES, COVER LETTERS, REFERENCES, & APPLICATIONS

ESSENTIAL CAREER ADVICE FOR THERAPY PROFESSIONALS

WHAT ARE SOME TIPS FOR WRITING MY RESUME?

When you sit down to write your resume, staring at the blank screen can be daunting. Start by not worrying about format, font, or fancy wording.

The most important part of your resume is your job history. Start by simply listing your employers and the dates you worked there. Then, add your education. Finally, add any additional relevant experiences (awards, honors, continuing education, etc.).

Once your categories are plainly listed and outlined, you can begin to fill in details such as practice setting and job responsibilities. Add your name, title, and contact information (including address) to the top of the page.

By taking it one step at a time, you should find that it's less overwhelming to get your resume written!

Once you've triple checked your resume for grammar and spelling, now you can add the personal touch you desire. Choose a plain, easy-to-read font and keep the size and style consistent.

Finally, ask a friend or two to look it over. Never skip on an extra set of eyes... you never know what you may have missed!

IS THERE A STANDARD FORMAT I SHOULD USE FOR MY RESUME?

A resume is as unique as the therapist it belongs to. There's no perfect equation that will guarantee a callback.

When you search resume formats online, you're opening up a whole can of worms. There are thousands of templates, websites offering resume advice, dos and don'ts. It can be overwhelming to say the least! One article will tell you to keep your resume under a page in length, while another says that it's better to space it out and include more.

THE TRUTH?
A resume is not a one-size-fits-all kind of thing.

What the employer really cares about is your work history. Dates, practice settings, and company names are all you need. After that, what you do with your additional page (or two) is entirely up to you. Highlight your education, clinicals, continuing education, certifications, specialties, and anything else you believe may make you an attractive candidate. Also, make sure to include your contact information... that includes your current address.

Don't worry whether your name should be bold or if your phone number should be more to the left.

When creating and updating your resume, allow it to reflect you professionally, be honest, and go with your gut. That's all there is to it.

Career Tree Network

WHAT CATEGORIES OR TOPICS SHOULD I COVER ON MY RESUME?

A good resume will provide ample detail on the work experiences that you've had. An HR person reviews a resume to determine if the candidate is qualified for the position.

Qualifications will come primarily from work experience and educational attainment.

Focus your efforts on those two sections!

Other common sections on the resume include:

OBJECTIVE - tells the employer what you're looking for in a position.

EDUCATION - shares your educational history.

CERTIFICATIONS - overview of any professional certifications.

WHAT ORDER SHOULD THE CATEGORIES ON MY RESUME APPEAR?

An "objective" section fits nicely at the top of your resume to set the stage for your career aspirations. Related experience is a very important component to the overall resume. We recommend putting your "experience" section towards the top of your resume, under the "objective".

The section on your "educational background" could fit nicely immediately following the experience overview. Any other sections that you want to include should fall under the three that we've outlined above.

HOW LONG SHOULD MY RESUME BE?

Resume size does not matter. An old school of thought proposed that all resumes should be kept to one page in length. For some people, especially new grads or those with just a few years of experience, a one page resume will do just fine.

On the other hand for individuals with more work experience, an additional page might be needed to fully explain your career accomplishments and goals.

As a general rule, your resume should be no more than 3 pages. If you have more information to share, such as reference information or a list of continuing education completed, you can create supplemental documents, available upon request.

Recruiters and Hiring Managers typically want to hire people with clear and concise communication skills. A well-written resume will showcase your key qualifications while keeping the information easy to read and to the point.

WHAT DOES A GOOD OBJECTIVE STATEMENT LOOK LIKE?

The objective statement is used to grab the attention of the HR professional. Most recruiters will only spend between 10 and 30 seconds reviewing your resume. It is vital that you make a good first impression.

Your objective should be your clearly written short term career goal.

EXAMPLE: I aspire to secure a full-time position as an Outpatient Occupational Therapist near Milwaukee, Wisconsin.

WHAT KEYWORDS SHOULD I USE IN MY RESUME?

Based on the opening you're applying for, you want to use keywords that directly relate to that setting or niche that the position would fall into.

For example, if you're applying to an Outpatient position, you want to be sure to have "Outpatient" somewhere on your resume.

When it comes to certifications, it's okay to use abbreviations, but you should also be sure to spell it out just in case an employer runs a keyword search on your resume. It's always important to include your job title, such as Physical Therapist, especially when uploading your resume online.

In general, keywords aren't too important in therapy because only a small number of therapists apply to any given position. Employers tend to manually look at each resume rather than running keyword searches.

WHAT ARE THE TOP MISTAKES I SHOULD AVOID IN A RESUME?

One mistake that people often make is having an unnecessarily long or wordy resume. As a general rule, your resume should be a maximum of two or three pages in length. You should be able to articulate your experience clearly and concisely.

Grammar and spelling errors, though highly discouraged and often talked about, are among the top mistakes people make when writing a resume. Not only should you scan your resume for errors, but you should ask at least one other person to check for mistakes, misspellings, and inaccuracies. These small mistakes can communicate to employers that you are not detail-oriented, or that you don't take the time to review your work.

If your resume is too specific, or your objective statement doesn't relate to the job you're applying for, it will often be discounted and discarded.

IS THERE ANYTHING I SHOULD LEAVE OUT OF MY RESUME?

There are plenty of things you should leave out of your resume. Your resume exists to show potential employers your work history, education, skills, and attributes.

While the format of your resume can vary greatly while remaining professional, there are certain details to avoid no matter what.

It's not necessary, and can actually hurt your chances, to include personal information such as your family and marital status, overly personal details like unrelated hobbies, pictures, and physical attributes.

Many people list "references available upon request," but it's better to leave this overused line off of your resume. Employers are constantly looking at resumes. They are well aware that they can request your references at any given point.

HOW SHOULD I SEND MY RESUME TO EMPLOYERS? FAX? E-MAIL? SNAIL MAIL? APPLY ONLINE?

Most employers will have a preferred method for how they want candidates to submit resumes. For hard-to-fill positions, like many healthcare positions, employers will be more flexible and happy to receive your resume by any method. For other positions, you'll need to follow the instructions to get your resume in the hopper.

Then once submitted, we recommend doing a series of proactive contacts to push your resume through the system. This proactive approach can vary based on how much time you have and how badly you want the job.

I'M A PHYSICAL THERAPIST LOOKING FOR A NEW JOB. SHOULD I POST MY RESUME ONLINE?

Posting your resume online is an easy, and somewhat low risk avenue to have employers contact you about potential job opportunities.

Rather than going out and researching companies and open positions...by posting your resume online, you're allowing the jobs to come to you.

The downside is that only jobs that are difficult to fill will come to you. If a job has many applicants and is quite popular, the employer will not spend time searching a resume database.

As a result, if you're a therapy professional who is somewhat flexible with your career search, online resume databases are a great, low-risk place to start. On the other hand, if you've got your heart set on a particular set of requirements in a popular geographic location, posting your resume online likely won't be of much help.

Most resume databases are free (for job seekers), so the downside is pretty minimal.

SIDE NOTE: If you haven't discussed with your employer about your job search and they come across your resume online, you could potentially face termination or awkward tensions at work.

For the most part, posting your resume online is an easy way to allow interested employers contact you with little effort on your part.

WHAT DO I NEED TO KNOW ABOUT APPLICANT TRACKING SYSTEMS?

Many employers use Applicant Tracking Systems (ATS) to help manage the hiring process. The systems can be somewhat clumsy for you, the candidate, to use because you'll have to fill out all of your information to be submitted into the ATS.

In theory, the Applicant Tracking System will keep the process moving along quickly.

You may receive automated email messages updating you on the status of the position. If you're applying online and you fill out an application, you're likely doing that through an ATS. Once your information is in the system, the employer can keep in touch for opportunities down the road.

Some Applicant Tracking Systems allow employers to search resumes based on keywords, so it's important to be sure that your resume is clear about who you are what your background is.

Career Tree Network

HOW CAN I MAKE MY RESUME STAND OUT TO REHAB MANAGERS?

Your resume is really a reflection of your work history. It's not a legal document, there's no set formatting or requirements that your resume has to meet. With that, in some ways, it's like a work of art that reflects your work history and the skills that you would bring to the table.

You have an opportunity to really highlight the skills and background that you have to make you the best candidate for the job.

The goal of the resume is to show the employer why you are uniquely qualified for any position that you're applying for.

It can't be everything to everybody, so in some ways your resume doesn't have to be attractive to all types of people, but it should really sell you as a candidate for your skills and what you've accomplished professionally. Employers are looking at your work history and practice settings, give detail there in particular. Length of time and type of setting is the most important part.

As you're explaining work history, put more detail around what you've accomplished and what you'd bring to the table if hired.

ARE COVER LETTERS EVEN USED THESE DAYS? WHY SHOULD I BOTHER WITH IT?

A cover letter is your chance to stand out among applicants whose resumes look exactly like yours. When you're competing for a position with a pool of therapists who share similar experience and education, your cover letter can be what separates you from the rejection pile and the interview pile.

Cover letters are important assets that you can use to allow your experience to come to life. Whereas a resume lists generic details, like dates and titles, your cover letter can speak to your therapy and leadership experience on a deeper level.

If two candidates with the same experience apply for a position, but one provides a cover letter and the other doesn't, the employer will likely opt for the one with the cover letter.

WHAT CONTENT MAKES A COVER LETTER GREAT?

At the end of the day, a cover letter is really just sharing how you uniquely meet the qualifications of the position. If you look at the job advertisement, you can identify certain requirements listed and form an outline for your cover letter by matching your experience with each individual requirement.

It's a good idea to use the same language used in the job advertisement in order to show the employer that your experience matches the need.

It's also important to customize your cover letter for each position that you apply for. While you can have a standard template you recycle, you should be sure to edit the content to best match the individual position and organization you're applying to.

SHOULD MY RESUME AND COVER LETTER CONTAIN THE SAME INFORMATION?

No. Your cover letter and resume serve two distinct purposes. A resume is more of a standard summary of your professional experience; it's going to stay the same regardless of what position you're applying to. Your past is your past.

Your cover letter, on the other hand, shares why you are uniquely qualified for this particular job. It should explain why you're interested in this particular opening and why you're the best candidate. The cover letter is unique to the job and company to which you're applying.

Basically, your resume will remain the same from application to application while your cover letter will need to be customized.

Career Tree Network

WHAT SHOULD MY COVER LETTER INCLUDE? HOW LONG SHOULD IT BE?

Your cover letter should answer the question of why you're uniquely qualified for a position. It is also the place to explain anything that's unclear in the resume or application, such as your plans to relocate to a local address in the near future.

It's possible to include an explanation for any employment gaps in your cover letter, but it's better to list them directly on the resume, so that the employer can see an explanation as they review your work history.

A cover letter should be no more than three to four paragraphs maximum. Often, employers are not fully reading the cover letter verbatim, but it's still important to include.

Don't try to oversell yourself in the cover letter. Employers can see right through that. Allow your experience to speak for itself as the employer learns what skills you can offer.

DO I NEED TO WRITE A NEW COVER LETTER FOR EACH JOB I APPLY FOR?

Cover letters, like resumes, should be unique to the candidate applying. However, they should also be unique to the position.

There's no need to write a brand new cover letter for each position you apply for, but it is a good idea to personalize it for each employer. You can write a standard cover letter draft to include standard information you'd like to impress potential employers with, and then tweak it each time you apply for a new position.

The personalized points should highlight what skills you have that that particular employer values. For example, if you're applying for an opening in a Skilled Nursing setting, you'd want to edit your cover letter to emphasize your experience in geriatrics. The bulk of the document can stay the same, but you want to show off your strengths and how they might benefit the employer.

In your cover letter, you want to showcase why your resume deserves a shot. Employers want to know about your unique talents and how exactly you might fit in to their facility.

There's no need to write a new cover letter each time (much like a resume), but you do want to do some research and find out exactly who you're pitching to.

Career Tree Network

TO WHOM SHOULD I ADDRESS MY COVER LETTER?

Throughout the hiring process, your cover letter could be read by a number of individuals. It will likely be read first by a Human Resources professional, then a hiring manager, and potentially other members of the interview team.

When addressing the cover letter, it really depends on your preferences. You could say "To Whom it May Concern," or "Dear Hiring Manager."

As a rule of thumb, it's best to err on the side of more professionalism, so "Dear Hiring Manager," is probably the best way to address the letter.

WHAT SHOULD I AVOID SAYING IN MY COVER LETTER?

When writing your cover letter, you want to avoid rehashing your resume. The cover letter should share more in-depth information than what's listed out on your resume. There should be additional and different details.

You also want to avoid overselling yourself in your cover letter. Let your experience speak for itself. It can be easy to go too far when writing a cover letter, but if you focus on your experience and how that translates to the new position, you should be set.

Try not to appear overenthusiastic. Employers can see through that right away. If you're excited about a job, that's good and you can let that excitement show. But be sure to clearly name what it is about that employer or opening specifically that you're interested in.

DO EMPLOYERS CHECK REFERENCES? WHAT'S THE POINT?

If an employer believes you are a good fit for their facility, they will almost always contact at least two of your references. After a hiring manager has gotten to know you throughout the interview process, they've determined you'd make a good fit within their facility.

But it's hard to know how someone might actually fit in unless they hear it first-hand.

Employers engage with professional references to get an idea of what it's really like to work with you. Your references should be people who have seen you at work - former supervisors, clinical instructors, and coworkers who you have had a professional relationship with.

It's possible that a hiring manager thought you would be a great fit, but one of your references mentioned that you were often late to work, didn't take responsibility for your actions, or didn't get along with your coworkers. These are all things that employers look for.

They can also help push you over the edge (one way or another) if an employer was on the fence about whether or not to hire you.

References help employers determine whether a potential candidate would be a good employee based on whether they've been a good employee in the past.

WHO SHOULD I LIST AS REFERENCES?

References are an important part of the hiring process. Often, they're the last checkpoint you need to pass before receiving an offer.

Your references should be people who have seen you in a professional setting. They should not be friends or family, but people who can speak to your experience as a therapist. They should know you well enough to be able to speak on your behalf.

If you're fairly new to the field, clinical instructors and professors can be great references. Typically employers like to contact 2-3 references, but it's a good idea to have a few people on standby.

WHAT DO EMPLOYERS WANT FROM JOB REFERENCES?

When employers contact your references, they basically want to know whether you would be a good fit for the job. They want to know if you perform well, have an area of weakness that they need to be aware of, and whether they'll regret hiring you.

Reference checks are really more of a last checkpoint after the interview process is completed (and sometimes even after an offer has been extended) to determine whether hiring you would be a mistake. Typically, employers won't bother calling someone's references if they're not already interested in the candidate.

You can think of reference checks as the last hoop to jump through before an employer is totally sold.

HOW DO I GO ABOUT ASKING SOMEONE TO BE A REFERENCE?

When deciding who your references should be, remember that they should be people who have seen you in a professional setting, can vouch for your skills as a therapist, and are reliable communicators.

It's typical for most employers to request three references, but it's not a bad idea to have a few back-ups just in case.

Once you've identified who you'd like to ask, you should approach them in a professional manner. It's important to ask whether they would be comfortable answering questions about your professionalism and skills as a therapist. Be sure to ask what about their preferred contact methods and times they would be available so that the employer is easily able to reach them.

When you have applied for a position, be in contact with your references to give them a heads up that they might be receiving a call or an email. It's important to establish if they are still willing and available to speak on your behalf.

HOW CAN I PREPARE REFERENCES TO BE CONTACTED?

When you trust someone enough to ask them to vouch for you in the professional realm, you want to treat that relationship with care. After you've asked someone to be a reference for you, don't leave it there.

Each time you apply to a new job, reach out to your references to give them a heads up that they might be contacted by a particular employer.

It's important to give your references notice so they're not caught off guard. Maintaining regular contact with your references is a good idea. The reference check is typically one of the last steps in the interview process, so you'll want to be sure that your references are around and available to speak on your behalf.

WHAT QUESTIONS ARE ASKED DURING REFERENCE CHECKS?

Each employer has a different set of questions to ask your references, but they'll pretty much follow some general guidelines.

By this point in the process, you've made a good impression and the employer thinks you'll be a good fit... but they want someone else's opinion who's experienced your work firsthand.

EMPLOYERS WILL USUALLY ASK SOME VERSION OF THE FOLLOWING QUESTIONS:
1. What are the candidate's strengths as a therapist?
2. What is a weakness of the candidate's?
3. What is he/she like as a coworker/supervisor/employee?
4. Would you hire him/her again if given the chance?

Your references should know you on a professional level. When you're selecting people to be your references, keep in mind that the employer is just looking for another perspective on your professionalism and your work as a therapist.

Career Tree Network

IF I SUSPECT I HAVE A BAD REFERENCE, HOW DO I KEEP THEM FROM RUINING MY CAREER?

Most employers will not call your past employers without first obtaining your permission. The easiest way for you to avoid a bad reference is simply not listing that person as a reference.

Unless you've given specific references from your previous job, it's likely that the potential employer would not contact that particular person or workplace about you.

It's a good idea to update your references as you progress in your career so that potential employers are receiving the most accurate, up-to-date information about your work history.

IS THERE INFORMATION A FORMER EMPLOYER OR EX-BOSS CANNOT GIVE OUT?

Most former employers and ex-bosses do not have a personal vendetta against you. They're not going to go out of their way to share negative information about you or your work history.

If you've listed them as a reference, the prospective employer can ask them any question they want, but it varies by employer.

Depending on interpersonal relationships, if your prospective employer has a friendship with your former employer, they might be able to learn additional details about how you were as an employee.

Some employers have a policy not to give out reference information or salary history, but for the most part nothing is off limits.

HOW DO I THANK A GOOD REFERENCE AFTER LANDING THE JOB?

References can be the make-it or break-it aspect of the hiring process. Many employers who are on the fence about whether or not to hire someone, make their decisions based on what their references have to say.

That being said, when you land a new position you should go out of your way to thank the references who got you there!

You can offer to return the favor if and when they begin looking for a new position. It's also a good idea to keep them informed about the new position. You can follow up after your first few days, weeks, and months at a new workplace and let your references know how their recommendation has impacted your career.

WHAT ARE SOME TIPS FOR A SUCCESSFUL JOB APPLICATION?

When filling out an online job application, you may not be allotted much room for details. Therefore, accuracy is the most important thing.

Employers post job applications in order to easily identify applicants who aren't qualified for the position. Be sure to thoroughly read the job description and requirements before taking the time to apply.

On an application, keep your answers concise and honest. Often, you will have the option to upload your resume. The resume and application are designed to complement one another, so be sure that the two are consistent. You don't need to repeat verbatim what you've already written on your resume, but the answers should match up.

Before submitting, be sure that you've filled out each and every question. It's easy to overlook something small that could ultimately cost you the job.

Career Tree Network

HOW CAN I GET AN EMPLOYER TO RESPOND TO A JOB APPLICATION?

To put it simply, employers often move quickly when a candidate has another job offer on the table. The theory is that if another organization is offering a someone a position, that candidate has proven his or her value and is therefore worthy of a more timely consideration.

Basically, if one organization likes a candidate, it makes the employer think that they should take a closer (and quicker) look at the candidate as well.

The best way to move the hiring process along quickly is to get an offer in hand, go back to the places you've applied, and share that you are very interested, but have another offer that you need to respond to. Ask the employer what their timeline is to see if it would work out for you to interview with them.

Generally speaking, it's easiest to get an offer for a position in a more remote geographic area. If you apply to positions in a less desirable location or practice setting, you can not only gain practice in interviewing, but you can also obtain job offers that you can then use in negotiation for positions that you really want.

WHAT ARE COMMON MISTAKES WITH ONLINE APPLICATIONS?

Online applications are a great way to speed up the hiring process... but they do come with downsides of their own. When filling out applications online, it's easy to make mistakes. You really have to be vigilant when typing your work history, checking boxes, and submitting your materials online.

Online applications can also be less personal. While most employers use an online application system now, you want to take additional measures to stand out from the other names and resumes floating across their screen.

AFTER I SUBMIT MY RESUME AND APPLICATION FOR A JOB, HOW DOES AN EMPLOYER EVALUATE IT?

Employers are looking to see what experience you have and how that relates to their setting and open position. They want to know how your past work/clinical experience would compare to their setting and the skills that you would need to bring to the table.

A secondary factor that employers look at is whether it makes sense for you to come and work for them based on geographic location. If you are applying for a job in Atlanta, but you live in Milwaukee, they're going to question why you're applying to their organization.

Within your cover letter and application materials, it's important that you clarify any discrepancies around why you're applying for this position. If you're planning on relocating, make sure that the employer doesn't have to search very hard to see that.

You also want to make sure that your resume and application materials show your best work and clinical history, so that the employer is easily able to identify that you would be a good fit for the position.

WHAT CAN I DO TO ENSURE THAT MY APPLICATION DOESN'T GET LOST IN THE SHUFFLE?

The secret to success is being able to follow up without becoming annoying.

In the case that you're genuinely interested in a position, it's in your best interest to go above and beyond simply submitting an application online. You should be following up via phone and email to ensure that your materials were received and to see if the employer has any follow-up questions.

When submitting an application, it's important to be as clear as possible about why you're uniquely qualified for the job. Your cover letter is a great place to set yourself apart from a generic online form.

Remember that employers operate on different timelines, so you may not hear back for a period of time. That doesn't mean they're not interested, but they do have other priorities, so patience is important.

If you've submitted your best materials and have followed up, you can relax, wait patiently and trust that you will hear back at some point.

Career Tree Network

200 WORDS

INTERVIEWS

ESSENTIAL CAREER ADVICE FOR THERAPY PROFESSIONALS

HOW MANY ROUNDS OF INTERVIEWS CAN I EXPECT? ON THE PHONE, IN PERSON...

In a typical hiring process, most employers tend to conduct one phone interview and one in-person interview. Both rounds of interviews are equally important to show the employer that you are professional, interested, and qualified for the position. Often, your in-person interview will not be with the same person who interviewed you over the phone.

There could also be an additional in-person interview or job shadow, depending on the outcome of the original interviews. However, it's most common to just have two rounds of formal interviews.

WHAT BEHAVIORS DO EMPLOYERS LOOK FOR IN THE INTERVIEW?

During the interview process, employers are looking to see how your past work experience and behavior would relate to the job that they have available.

Typically, they'll ask behavioral-based interview questions and ask you to talk about a time in the past that you've done certain things or had certain experiences.

"TELL ME A TIME WHEN ..."

The theory behind this kind of behavioral interviewing is that past experiences and behaviors can potentially equate to future results and behaviors.

The employer is looking for examples of how you've reacted to certain situations and experiences in an attempt to determine compatibility with their organization and the job opening.

They will also be looking at nonverbal communication. Examples of this are whether you bring your cell phone into the interview, make eye contact, or have dirt under your fingernails.

Basically, the interviewer is looking for different cues that might relate to who you are and how you would perform on the job.

Career Tree Network

SHOULD I PRACTICE FOR AN INTERVIEW? IF SO, HOW?

One of the best ways to prepare for an interview is to practice with someone else. Ask a friend, classmate, or coworker to come up with a list of mock interview questions. Not only does practicing with someone else give you an opportunity to think through your answers, but it also gives you an opportunity to receive feedback.

Ask your fake interviewer to point out any nervous habits (think: um, like, uh, you know?) and then, when you go through the questions a second time, focus on eliminating those fillers.

Once you've gone through the interview two or three times, you'll feel more confident about what kind of questions might be asked and how you might respond.

Another good way to practice for your interview is to find a list of common questions within your discipline and type out your responses. This forces you to take your time forming a complete answer. Read over your responses a few times before the interview and you'll feel as prepared as possible!

WHAT'S THE BEST WAY TO PREPARE FOR A JOB INTERVIEW?

When you applied for the position, you probably saw a job description that highlighted the major responsibilities and requirements of the position. Spend time reading that job description to ensure that you fully understand all that the position entails.

The description will list requirements and also desired traits of the ideal candidate.

REQUIREMENT = Candidate hired must have this.
DESIRED = Would be nice for candidate to have this, but not 100% necessary.

If you lack a certain requirement, proactively develop an action plan on how you will make up for it. For example, if the position requires CPR certification, learn the steps involved to get certified. Then during the interview, be quick to point out that while you don't have the certification you would be able to obtain certification within a short time frame.

When talking with the interview team, you should focus on how your skills and experience match with the traits of their ideal candidate.

The goal of the interview is to determine if candidates can successfully perform job responsibilities. With an understanding of the job description, you will then be able to prove that you have the necessary skills and experiences to excel in the position.

Career Tree Network

HOW SHOULD I RESEARCH AN ORGANIZATION BEFORE THE JOB INTERVIEW?

First off, bravo for even thinking about researching the employer before an interview. It's an important topic that most people don't do.

The goal with your research should be to gain an understanding of the facility and overall organization. You should also closely review the job description to explore the requirements/responsibilities.

HERE ARE SOME SPECIFIC AVENUES TO EXPLORE:
1. Visit the company website and spend time reviewing the information.
2. Use social networking websites like Twitter, Facebook and LinkedIn to build connections with key employees and follow the company profiles.
3. Subscribe for email alerts on press releases and other official company communications.
4. Seek to understand the culture of the organization including challenges facing the organization and industry.
5. Search on-line reviews from patients to get a feel for how it operates.
6. Track down current and former employees to see what it's like to work there.
7. Read newspaper articles about the company and its key organizational leaders.

The goal here is to become a quasi expert on the organization. Properly conducting this type of research will be a little time consuming, but it will pay off when you impress the interview team with your knowledge.

WHAT IS THE PROCESS AN EMPLOYER TYPICALLY FOLLOWS TO MAKE A JOB OFFER?

After all of their prospective interviews are completed, a hiring team will typically get together to discuss the interested candidates. This can take a while based on the schedules of the team and how urgent the hiring need.

This can cause a delay in receiving a job offer. Don't be discouraged if it takes a while to hear back. There are a number of reasons you may not have been contacted yet.

Generally speaking, the job offer is extended after references and background checks are completed. You will usually receive a phone call that outlines the details of the offer. The phone call will typically be followed up with additional information via email.

Within the offer, the employer will share important details including wage, benefits, start date, etc. Don't be shy about asking for additional information if you feel that it's necessary to make a decision. There is no need to accept an offer immediately; feel free to take some time to think things over.

Career Tree Network

WHAT SHOULD I KNOW ABOUT PHONE INTERVIEWS?

The main thing to remember about phone interviews is that they are your first impression to the interviewer and should be taken seriously. Phone interviews are often very brief.

The goal of a phone interview for the employer is to make sure that you as the candidate, meet the minimum qualifications for the job and are actually interested in the job.

There will be more specific and in-depth questions in the in-person interview, but the phone interview is just as important as any other step in the hiring process.

HOW CAN I IMPRESS A POTENTIAL EMPLOYER OVER THE PHONE?

The first step in impressing a potential employer over the phone is to recognize that the phone call you're receiving is an interview. You should take the call in a spot where you're prepared and comfortable having a professional conversation. If you are driving, watching TV, or in a place with a lot of background noise, you would want to ask them to call you back when you are more available and prepared.

At that point, the interviewer may just try to complete the interview then and there, but it's in your best interest to try and reschedule.

One of the best things about phone interviews is that, because they can't see you, the employer doesn't know what resources you're utilizing. You can print off a copy of your resume, prepare questions in advance, and pull up the company website to reference during the conversation.

Your ability to use cheat sheets puts you at a distinct advantage during the phone interview.

WHAT ARE SOME SKILLS I NEED IN ORDER TO ACE AN INTERVIEW?

The most important thing you can bring to an interview is confidence. Developing a level of confidence in the skills and experience that you possess is important. Remember: you are interviewing the employer as much as they are interviewing you. It's a two-way street.

Trust that your skills are valuable. Having confidence to portray yourself in a favorable light is going to distinguish you from other interviewees. If you're not convinced that your skills and background are assets, why should the employer?

Prior to the interview, you also want to review your interpersonal skills and make sure that you don't have any nonverbal traits that would distract from the employer's ability to fully consider you for the position. Things like dressing appropriately, having good posture, and maintaining eye contact are all important aspects to communicate your professionalism.

WHAT INFORMATION CAN I EXPECT EMPLOYERS TO GIVE ME PRIOR TO AN INTERVIEW?

In general, employers want you to be successful during the interview process. They don't want to have to interview more people than necessary. Most employers will provide you a basic outline such as where to go for the interview, where to park, and who to ask for.

Above and beyond that, you'll have to do research online and ask around to get a better feel for the organization and what they're all about. It's always a good idea to arrive to the interview with knowledge about the organization.

HOW SHOULD I DRESS FOR MY INTERVIEW?

This point is really simple: **always dress for success.**

If you have a suit, wear the suit. Make sure that there are no noticeable stains on the outfit. Wear an extra layer of deodorant or antiperspirant to eliminate body odors. Brush your teeth before the interview or bring a mint.

If you are coming to the interview from work or a clinical, it would be best to make a pit stop and change to your dress outfit prior to the scheduled interview.

BE SURE TO DRESS CONSERVATIVELY. You may want to wear clothing that covers up tattoos.

It looks extra professional if you bring a notebook / portfolio and pen to the interview for taking notes during the conversation. You can also have some of your questions for the hiring team and any notes that you may have taken based on your pre-interview research inside your portfolio.

Leave your cell phone in the car, or put it on silent mode.

Employers like to see that the candidate cares enough about the opportunity to show up to the interview on time and dressed in a professional manner. This is one small way to crease a solid first impression with the interview team.

WHAT IS THE MOST COMMON INTERVIEW MISTAKE MADE BY THERAPY PROFESSIONALS?

From your perspective, the primary goal of the interview should be to sell the employer that you're the best candidate to fill their open position.

As a secondary goal, you'll want to take time during the interview to learn about the employer and the open job so that you can determine if the position is a match for your career aspirations.

BOTH ARE IMPORTANT.
You need to sell the employer...and to some extent, the employer needs to sell you.

The most common mistake, especially for therapy professionals, is to come in and start right of the bat with negotiations and making demands of the employer. "I can only work until 3pm on Tuesdays." "I know you have a location in XXXXX, but I'm not willing to go there." "I'll only treat orthopedic patients, if we have other patients someone else will need to do that." "How much will you pay me?" etc.

As you might imagine, candidates who begin with demands or restrictions are not seen in a favorable light. We all have some preferences, but those should be shared later in the interview process...and after the employer has decided that you're the best candidate for the job.

WHAT ARE SOME QUESTIONS AN HR PROFESSIONAL MIGHT ASK ME DURING AN INTERVIEW?

The HR professional or recruiter is primarily looking to assess whether or not you meet the minimum position requirements. Here are some common questions that an HR professional / recruiter might ask:

- How many years of experience do you have as a therapy professional?
- Why are you looking to leave your current employer?
- What are you looking for in your next position?
- What are some areas where you lack experience or training?
- Is it ever acceptable to lie to a patient? If yes, under what circumstances?
- When did you first learn about our company?
- Would you recommend your last employer as a good place to work? Why or why not?
- What is your personal mission statement?
- Think back to a time when you had to be assertive. What was the situation? How did you handle it?
- If this was your company, would you hire yourself? Why?
- Where do you see yourself in five years?
- What is your greatest achievement?
- Disagreements with co-workers happen often, have you ever experienced this? How did the situation get resolved?
- What would past managers/supervisors say about you?
- Why are you the best person for this position?

HOW CAN I IMPRESS A HUMAN RESOURCES MANAGER DURING THE INTERVIEW PROCESS?

There are so many opportunities to impress throughout the interview process!

THESE ARE SOME OF THE MOST IMPORTANT THINGS THAT HUMAN RESOURCES MANAGERS LOOK FOR IN INTERVIEWEES:

- Interviewee is knowledgeable about the company
- Has questions to ask at the end of the interview
- Shows enthusiasm for the role
- Dresses professionally
- Is on time
- Uses proper phone etiquette
- Is flexible and accessible
- Brings a resume and references to the interview
- Asks about the next steps

Career Tree Network

WHAT ARE SOME QUESTIONS THAT I MIGHT BE ASKED AT THE START OF A JOB INTERVIEW?

Interviews usually start with a few questions about your background. These questions are fairly straight forward and help give the interview team a good understanding of your work history and educational experiences. If you have a good understanding of your resume, you will probably be well prepared to answer these questions. The interviewer will have already read your resume, so make every effort to share background without simply rehashing your resume.

EDUCATION
1. Thinking back to your time in school, what were some of your favorite classes?
2. Did you participate in any special projects or research opportunities?
3. What skills would you like to develop in the next six months?
4. How would you describe your learning style?

EXPERIENCE
1. Why are you looking to leave your current employer?
2. What are some of your clinical strengths?
3. What are some of your clinical weaknesses?
4. Why did you choose _____ as a career?
5. What do you like most about working with a _____ population?

WHAT ARE SOME THOUGHT PROVOKING QUESTIONS THAT I MIGHT BE ASKED DURING A JOB INTERVIEW?

These questions typically have no right or wrong answers. Within these questions your thoughts and feelings are observed in an effort to learn more about your personality and approach to patient care.

ORGANIZATION
1. How should an organization support the professional development of its employees?
2. What type of environment do you feel fosters the best patient recovery?
3. What does "patient focused care" mean to you?

CAREER ASPIRATIONS
1. Why do you want to work for us?
2. What is your greatest achievement?
3. Some people have a "thirst for knowledge." Does this describe you? Why or why not?

PERSONALITY
1. Who are your heroes? Who do you admire?
2. Is it ever acceptable to lie to a patient? If yes, under what circumstances?
3. If you could choose one superhero power, what would it be and why?

QUALITY OF WORK
1. Why should we hire you over the others waiting to be interviewed?
2. Who has impacted you most in your career, how?
3. List five words that describe your personality.

Career Tree Network

WHAT IS BEHAVIORAL BASED INTERVIEWING?

Behavioral based interviewing questions have become extremely popular in the last 10 years. The idea is that past behavior is an indicator of future success. People who performed well in the past will also perform well in the future, and poor performers will also be poor in the future. The goal of this approach is to learn how you actually handled situations in previous work experiences. In some cases, you will also be asked to share examples from your personal life.

Interviewers are looking for actual experiences that you have had, so be very specific about what you did and how you handled the various situations. As you prepare for these questions, you may want to create a list of experiences that you can refer to during the interview.

WHAT ARE SOME BEHAVIORAL BASED QUESTIONS THAT MIGHT BE ASKED DURING AN INTERVIEW?

With the right amount of planning and preparation, you can become a shining star in the eyes of any interviewer. Your preparation should include reviewing these behavioral questions and maybe even asking a friend to role play for a mock interview. Remember to provide specific examples.

QUALITY OF WORK
1. Think back to a time when a patient thanked you for a job well done. What was the situation? What did the patient say?
2. Tell me about an idea that you had which saved time or made your job easier.
3. What would past patients say about your treatment style?

INTERPERSONAL SKILLS
1. Have you ever dealt with a family member who interfered with your ability to treat a patient? What was the situation? How did you handle it?
2. Disagreements with co-workers happen often, have you ever experienced this? How did the situation get resolved?
3. Have you ever had a demanding supervisor or clinical instructor? What happened?

GOAL ACCOMPLISHMENT
1. Talk about a time you faced adversity to achieve a goal.
2. What is one new skill you learned in the last year?
3. What is the hardest goal you ever accomplished?

AS THE INTERVIEW COMES TO A CLOSE, WHAT ARE SOME QUESTIONS THAT MIGHT BE ASKED?

The last part of the interview will typically consist of a few simple yet important questions. Save some energy and brain power to give intelligent answers. This is the final stretch of the interview and these questions will separate you from the other candidates.

REQUIREMENTS & PREFERENCES:
1. What other organizations are you considering?
2. Do you have a target date in mind on when you'd like to start in a new position?
3. How long have you been looking for a position?
4. What are your salary requirements?

NEXT STEPS:
1. May we contact your references?
2. What additional information do you need to further research us?
3. Is there anything else that you'd like to share?
4. What questions do you have for me?

WHEN THE INTERVIEWER ASKS IF I HAVE ANY QUESTIONS, WHAT SHOULD I SAY?

You should have 5-7 questions prepared in advance and ready to ask of the interview team. Each person you meet will ask if you have any questions. Most candidates say something like, "Nope, I believe you've answered all my questions." This is not a professional response.

Accepting a new position is a BIG decision. You should have questions so that you can learn about the job and employer.

HERE ARE SOME SAMPLE QUESTIONS YOU MIGHT WANT TO ASK:

How are new employees orientated to the organization?
A good organization will ensure that you are comfortable. They will view the new employee orientation as a process rather than a one-hour event.

What characteristics does the ideal candidate possess?
Later when you write a thank you card/email, explain how your experience, education and personality match with their ideal candidate.

How is career growth supported at this organization?
This question shows that you are committed to grow and develop your skills.

How much turnover has there been among the therapy staff?
Happy employees do not leave.

What are the next steps in the interview process?
Asking this question, reaffirms your interest in the position and sets the stage for future dialog.

Career Tree Network

HOW SHOULD I ANSWER THE QUESTION OF WHERE I SEE MYSELF IN FIVE YEARS?

As you sit down for the job interview the sweat begins. You've done your homework, but there is still some apprehension around what questions will be asked and more importantly how to answer those questions. The fear is natural and with the right amount of antiperspirant, your anxiety will probably go unnoticed.

There's one famous interview question that many people dread.

SO...WHERE DO YOU SEE YOURSELF IN FIVE YEARS?

No need to fear, here's a good answer:

As a therapy professional, I would like to develop my skill set. In five years, I would like to be recognized as a leader in the field and to be seen as an expert. I feel that through this position, I will have an opportunity to do so.

WHAT'S THE EASIEST WAY TO SHOW MY GENUINE INTEREST DURING THE JOB INTERVIEW?

An interview must be viewed as a two-way street. The organization wants to learn about you and you want to learn about the organization. It's a mutual sharing exercise.

The best way to learn about the organization and to show your genuine interest, is to ask questions during your interview.

When a candidate asks questions during an interview, it shows that they have a solid interest in the company and position. If you fail to ask questions, the interview team will assume that you don't really want to work for the organization.

Asking questions shows that you're taking the interview seriously. You can ask questions about the position, organizational culture, patient population, practice specialties, technology / equipment utilized, members of the management team, growth strategies, benefits package, etc.

Develop a list of questions ahead of time and be sure to ask questions to each person that you meet. Bring a notebook and pen to take notes based on the answers.

You should have a list of between 5 to 7 questions prepared in advance and be sure to ask each person you meet 2 or 3 questions from your list.

Career Tree Network

WHAT ARE SOME QUESTIONS A REHAB MANAGER MIGHT ASK ME DURING AN INTERVIEW?

The Rehab Manager is mainly looking to assess a candidate's clinical skills. Here are some common questions that a Rehab Manager might ask:

- Have you worked with a _____ population? (insert Geriatric, Pediatric, etc.)
- How have you taken time to develop your skills in the last year?
- What do you least enjoy about working with a _____ population?
- What do you like most about working with a _____ population?
- What type of environment do you feel fosters the best patient recovery?
- What does "patient focused care" mean to you?
- How important is collaboration in a Rehab Department?
- How can technology enhance patient care?
- What's the most important thing you learned in school?
- What would past patients say about your treatment style?
- Tell me about an idea that you had which saved time or made your job easier.
- Have you ever dealt with a family member who interfered with your ability to treat a patient? What was the situation? How did you handle it?
- What is one new skill that you've learned in the last year?
- Did you participate in any special projects or research opportunities?
- What are some of your clinical strengths?
- What are some of your clinical weaknesses?

HOW CAN A THERAPY PROFESSIONAL IMPRESS A REHAB MANAGER DURING THE INTERVIEW PROCESS?

Rehab Managers are impressed by authentic passion. Stay away from cookie cutter answers and cliches that you can find online, and present the interviewer with genuine answers.

Give thought to your responses and show the interviewer that you mean what you say. When you are passionate about what you do, it means that you are willing and eager to learn and grow as a therapist, which is universally impressive.

WHAT QUESTIONS ARE ILLEGAL TO ASK ME IN AN INTERVIEW?

There are certain laws that dictate the hiring process and outline what areas an employer can or cannot ask about. Many personal items are off limits, such as marital status, whether you have or are planning to have children, sexual orientation, and race.

If an employer doesn't realize that these topics are off limits and asks you, for example, whether you're planning on having kids, it can create tension within the relationship and interview process.

In the case that you're asked something you're uncomfortable with, it's best to say something along the lines of "I'm not sure right now," or "I haven't thought much about that."

IT'S BEEN A WHILE SINCE MY INTERVIEW AND I HAVEN'T HEARD ANYTHING. WHAT SHOULD I DO?

FOLLOW UP!

Unfortunately, there's no scientific approach to hiring. Sometimes, an employer might be on the fence about whether or not to hire someone. If you're waiting in limbo and decide to follow up, one of two things might happen:

- They didn't want to hire you to begin with, so following up doesn't impact their decision.
- They did like you and were on the fence about hiring you, and following up reinforces that you're still interested in the opportunity.

By this logic, following up can't hurt you, but it can increase your probability of landing the position.

Career Tree Network

HOW CAN I IMPRESS A PRIVATE PRACTICE OWNER DURING THE INTERVIEW PROCESS?

While each employer varies on choosing personalities to work in their practice, a common thread is that private practice owners are looking for therapists to be service-oriented, honest, and authentic.

Let your experience speak for yourself throughout the interview process; there's no need to try and oversell your ability or personality. Just be who you are. This is the best way to determine whether there is a mutual fit.

Do not forget to do your homework. Most applicants are well-prepared and you want to be sure to appear professional and knowledgeable. Come in with a positive attitude, dress professionally, know about the organization, and articulate your goals.

I JUST COMPLETED THE INTERVIEW AND I REALLY WANT THIS JOB. WHAT SHOULD I DO NOW?

After the interview, plan to follow-up with each member of the interview team.

If you met five people during your site visit, then each of the five people should get a thank you card or email. Many candidates don't send thank you notes, so this extra effort sets you apart from other job seekers.

While you are at the clinic for the interview, obtain business cards or write down names of the interview team, this will make the post-interview follow-up easier.

During the interview, determine when they will make a decision and get a good feel for their timeline.

It will be your responsibility to maintain a good relationship with your primary contact. You may need to send an occasional email or place follow-up phone calls. The ball is always in your court and post-interview follow-up reaffirms your sincere interest.

FOLLOW-UP STEPS:
1. Send thank you cards to each person you met during the interview.
2. Go to social media and follow or like the organization profile pages.
3. Call or email the employer about a week later to confirm your interest and check the status.
4. Maintain contact with the people listed as your references to see if the employer has called them.

Career Tree Network

200 WORDS

RESIDENCY PROGRAMS

ESSENTIAL CAREER ADVICE FOR THERAPY PROFESSIONALS

WHAT SHOULD I EXPECT OUT OF A RESIDENCY PROGRAM?

Should you choose to become a resident in a residency program, you should expect to improve your clinical reasoning skills, hands-on skills, and expand your differential diagnoses.

You will learn how to follow best practice, measure outcomes, and understand your financial impact on patients and the healthcare system alike. You will also learn to understand the literature, but not hide behind the literature. As you will find out, it is not just the literature but patient values and your own experience that plays into best practice.

You will learn to be both optimistic and critical. Finally, you will learn how to take our profession to the next level. Thus, it is extremely beneficial to continue your professional journey through residency and specialty board certification.

HOW DO I CHOOSE THE BEST RESIDENCY PROGRAM FOR ME?

There are many ways to find out about residencies in your area. Both traditional and non-traditional residency models exist. If you want to stay in the region you currently reside in, ask your local clinics if they offer a residency program.

Non-traditional models typically allow you to join the team and begin a residency simultaneously. Traditional models may require you to search outside your current region to relocate for the opportunity.

Generally, with the traditional model, clinics will set aside a certain number of positions each year for an incoming cohort. For some, this may be the ideal situation and as a result, you may travel out of your region for this experience. The decision between these two models is obviously a personal decision depending on your life circumstances and career preferences.

If you choose a more non-traditional route, seek out the culture that fits you the best. If you find the right fit, you will play a role in further stabilizing that clinic's cultural excellence.

WHAT IS THE PROCESS FOR GETTING INTO THE RESIDENCY PROGRAM I WANT?

It is standard practice for residency programs to accept applications online. For many other programs, you can apply on RF-PTCAS. Once you have chosen a model that best matches your goals and fits your lifestyle, find the best residency programs within this model.

Each residency program that you choose will have its own application process. Contact the program directors and inquire about their process.

HOW CAN I BE SUCCESSFUL IN A RESIDENCY PROGRAM?

To be successful in a residency program, you need to be ready for adult learning. To do this, you must understand your strengths and weaknesses.

In order to feel that you've been successful in your residency program, you should aim to incorporate what you learn into your practice as quickly as possible, gain an understanding of strong clinical reasoning skills and use these skills to generalize your knowledge between multiple patient types. Practice your hands-on skills often. Finally, be prepared to be challenged!

WHAT ARE THE NEXT STEPS TO TAKE AFTER A RESIDENCY PROGRAM?

There are many subsequent steps and potential career paths that open up after a residency program. What path you choose is up to your own interests, strengths, and motivations.

Completion of a residency program as well as attaining a board-certified specialty can greatly improve your resume. You may find a plethora of opportunities that can arise, for example, overseeing other residency programs, teaching, and mentoring. Many companies will train their newly board-certified specialists to be mentors to incoming residents.

There are many clinicians that gain their board-certified specialty upon graduation. If you fit this bill, you may want to look at program development and/or improving clinical pathways at your place of employment. Many graduates will also consider fellowships to continue striving towards clinical excellence.

200 WORDS

WORKING WITH RECRUITERS

ESSENTIAL CAREER ADVICE FOR THERAPY PROFESSIONALS

WHAT ROLE DOES A RECRUITER OR HR MANAGER TYPICALLY PLAY WITHIN THE HIRING PROCESS?

Recruiters are responsible for locating, identifying, and building relationships with therapy candidates for current and future openings. They do this primarily by learning about the candidate and what they're looking for in their next opportunity.

Recruiters learn about the candidate's career goals and preferences such as setting, population, environment, FTE status, ideal location, etc. They are also responsible for scheduling interviews and giving candidates updates on the current status of the hiring process during the interview and job shadow stages.

WHAT DOES A RECRUITER OR HR MANAGER TYPICALLY LOOK FOR WHEN HIRING A THERAPY PROFESSIONAL?

Recruiters typically look for the following qualities in candidates:

- Clinical experience
- Experience within the setting (not always required, but definitely a plus!)
- Solid work history without a lot of short-term employment

As a rule, in the hiring process we look for the quality rather than quantity of experience. We are interested in what you could possibly bring to the table and we look to the solidity of your clinical experience to show us that.

WHY DO EMPLOYERS USE STAFFING AGENCIES?

In the healthcare industry, an organization will use staffing agencies when they struggle to find candidates on their own for an opening. The open position might be a permanent long-term need at the facility or a temporary short-term position to cover an illness, vacation, or maternity leave.

A staffing agency is especially helpful to find a candidate open to a short-term position. Nearly all healthcare employers struggle to cover short term staffing needs internally.

Due to the high cost involved, most employers would prefer to hire a candidate directly (without the help of an agency).

Employers may struggle to hire their own therapy professionals due to a number of reasons. The most common is a lack of local candidates within their area. Other reasons may include ineffective recruitment strategies, high turnover among staff, or a toxic work environment.

For a permanent placement position, the staffing agencies will earn a flat fee or percentage of your first year salary. For a travel / temporary position, the staffing agency will earn a margin of each hour that you work.

Most employers view staffing agencies as a last resort to avoid the fees involved (especially for permanent positions).

WHAT DO I NEED TO KNOW ABOUT RECRUITMENT AND STAFFING AGENCIES?

Recruitment and staffing agencies work on behalf of employers to help find candidates for short or long term hiring needs. Typically these organizations earn all their revenue from the employer and will NOT charge candidates for their services.

A staffing agency might need a candidate to cover a short-term travel assignment, like a maternity leave... or a long-term assignment where a therapist would work at an organization while they hire a permanent employee. (The standard length is typically 13 weeks.)

An agency could also be used to find a regular hire permanent employee for an open position.

Most agencies do not receive any money until a therapist goes to work for an employer.

There are some recruitment agencies that work on a retained search model. Within retained search, the agency will be paid upfront and engaged directly with the employer to help find candidates for an open position. There is usually an additional payment made when a successful placement is made.

Due to the high cost involved, working with a 3rd party recruiter or staffing agency is often seen as a last resort, when other options are not available.

Career Tree Network

FROM A RECRUITER OR HR PERSPECTIVE WHAT ARE SOME COMMON PITFALLS THAT YOU'VE SEEN THERAPY PROFESSIONALS MAKE?

One of the most common pitfalls that candidates make is not considering a setting outside of their comfort zone. Therapists are encouraged to expand their job search outside of whatever setting they happen to have the most experience in.

Each setting has unique benefits that a lot of therapists overlook and it's a good idea to consider, research, and maybe even apply to positions that may be slightly different than past jobs you've held.

200 WORDS

SALARY CONVERSATIONS

ESSENTIAL CAREER ADVICE FOR THERAPY PROFESSIONALS

WHEN DO I BRING UP SALARY WITHIN THE INTERVIEW PROCESS?

Salary conversations are going to happen...it's inevitable. You're going to get paid for the work that you perform as a therapy professional.

Many therapists bring up salary too soon and this can be a big turnoff to potential employers... and you may even earn less money if an offer is eventually extended.

The best strategy when discussing salary is to wait until the employer brings it up....which will typically happen when an offer is extended.

The employer needs time to learn about your background and the skills you bring to the table. If they quote you a salary range before having an understanding of your unique skill set, the number will almost always be on the low end because they don't know anything about you.

As such, negotiations should happen after you've sold yourself as being uniquely qualified to fill their open position and both parties (ie: you and the employer) have determined that you would be the best fit for the position.

With the offer in hand, you now have the full picture of the compensation package and can negotiate accordingly.

WHAT IF THE JOB I WANT CAN'T OFFER THE SALARY I NEED?

Based on your research, you've already developed that baseline compensation level that you will need to earn. If the offered salary is coming up short, then you might have to walk away. Other opportunities will emerge and may be a better fit for your experience level. If the employer knows that you're willing to accept their original offer, why should they give you a higher amount? The key is to remain level headed and know your baseline. Often, an employer will increase an offer, only after you've decided to walk away.

REMEMBER: If an offer doesn't work out, there are other fish in the sea.

HOW DO I HANDLE MULTIPLE JOB OFFERS?

Having multiple job offers is a good problem to have.

The best way to handle the situation is to think about your career goals. Make a decision with those goals in mind. Think about which offer would be optimal for your career.

You can use competing job offers as a point of negotiation to choose the opportunity or employer that you like the best. By doing this, you could potentially negotiate a better wage, more PTO, etc.

It's important that you have open communication with employers about your timeline to ensure that you're respectful of their time and energy. Employers typically don't like to have offers looming out there, so by communicating effectively and honestly, they are either able to recruit for more candidates or have you start as soon as possible and end their search.

WHAT DOES A TYPICAL BENEFITS PACKAGE INCLUDE? WHAT ASPECTS OF THE BENEFITS PACKAGE ARE NEGOTIABLE, IF ANY?

A typical benefits package includes insurance, paid time off, retirement, and continuing education. However, the specifics of the benefits vary greatly from one organization to the next. The insurance could be health, dental, and/or vision.

If smaller organizations are not able to offer benefits, many of them will pay an additional stipend or higher wages in lieu of benefits. It's possible that they might offer a higher hourly rate to adjust for benefits not being offered.

While it may be possible to negotiate additional PTO or continuing education packages, insurance and retirement benefits are almost always non-negotiable.

Because each employer offers slightly different benefits packages, it's important to clarify what benefits you'll receive when starting a new position.

HOW SHOULD I NEGOTIATE MY SALARY?

If you don't know where you're going, it will be difficult to get there. Similarly, if you don't know what compensation package you want, it will be difficult to achieve it.

Many candidates enter a negotiation looking to get the largest starting salary possible. They seem to have the mindset, "I don't know how much money I want, but I do know that I want to super-size it."

YOU MUST DEVELOP A SPECIFIC TARGET BASED ON A GOOD AMOUNT OF RESEARCH.

Conducting research will give you the information you need to make your approach more educated and effective.

HERE ARE THREE WAYS TO RESEARCH SALARY:
1. Visit salary benchmarking websites, like Salary.com to research salary ranges for your position and location.
2. Meet with former college professors to help develop your salary expectations.
3. Network with colleagues or contact your professional association.

Based on your research, develop a specific dollar amount as the benchmark. You might want to develop two dollar amounts, one as the ideal target and a lower amount as a baseline. The baseline is the absolute lowest salary that you would accept.

WHAT OTHER FACTORS BESIDES SALARY DO I NEED TO CONSIDER WHEN NEGOTIATING COMPENSATION?

The figure on your bi-weekly paycheck is only one component of the overall compensation package offered by an employer. Other factors such as health insurance, life insurance, disability, stock options, yearly bonus, paid time off and continuing education assistance must also be taken into consideration. At some organizations, these other factors can also be negotiable.

Take a look at the full picture and gain a clear understanding of the total benefit that you would enjoy from an employer.

For example, Company A pays an employee $50,000 per year, but only offers a watered down health insurance plan and five days of paid vacation.

Company B pays an employee $45,000 per year, but offers a full-service comprehensive benefits package with 30 days of paid time off per year and top-notch insurance.

In this case, the "better" offer will depend on what value you place on the various components of the total package.

HOW CAN I NEGOTIATE MORE VACATION TIME?

Often it's not possible to negotiate additional vacation time or PTO based on company policies and equity among staff. To add more vacation days to your package is usually not an option.

However, the vacation time that's originally communicated is typically for employees who don't have much prior work experience. If you bring more work experience to the table, it's possible to negotiate an extra week of vacation or PTO based on what you're currently receiving.

IF I'M GIVEN AN OFFER THAT I LIKE, SHOULD I TAKE TIME TO THINK, GIVE A COUNTER-OFFER, OR ACCEPT IMMEDIATELY?

If you're happy with the job offer that's been extended to you, and you'd like to go ahead and work for the organization, you may as well accept the offer immediately. There's no need to drag the process along.

If you think, based on your research, that the salary is too low or other factors aren't what they should be in terms of schedule, benefits, etc., then you could potentially negotiate.

I AM UP FOR A PROMOTION TO BECOME A MANAGER. HOW DO I NEGOTIATE COMPENSATION AND BENEFITS?

The best way to negotiate is to have another offer on the table. It's the cleanest and easiest way to show your employer that your skills are valuable and desired by another organization.

Employers are most likely to respond when you show them what a competing organization is willing to offer you for your skills and experiences.

You can also research compensation and benefits packages on sites like Salary.com and Glassdoor.com to get a better idea of what you can ask for and what you should expect.

I HEAR THERAPY PROFESSIONALS ARE IN HIGH DEMAND, SO WHY HAVE MY WAGES BEEN STAGNANT?

As a general rule, employers typically pay their employees the least amount of money possible. This is not solely within healthcare, but rather just a fundamental business principle to keep wages low.

When a candidate is hired for an open position, their starting wage sets the bar for future wages with that employer. So, for example, if someone is hired at $40 per hour, any wage increases will be a percentage from that initial starting wage.

Although therapists are in high demand now, the wage that you're currently receiving was determined in large part upon your hire date and what was negotiated at that point.

Large salary increases are rare in healthcare, so it's likely that your current wage is within a few percentage points of your starting wage.

Due to the current demand for your skills, it's possible that employers in your area might now be paying higher wages or offering other incentives (sign-on bonuses, student loan repayment, etc.) to new therapists hired.

The best way to determine the current market rate for your skills is to obtain job offers for other positions and either accept another offer or use it for negotiation at your current employer.

Career Tree Network

200 WORDS

STARTING & WORKING IN A NEW JOB

ESSENTIAL CAREER ADVICE FOR THERAPY PROFESSIONALS

WHAT ARE THE MOST IMPORTANT THINGS TO CONSIDER BEFORE ACCEPTING A JOB OFFER?

When you've been extended a job offer, you'll probably get that gut feeling. Either you're excited or you're not. If you feel good about the position, there are several things you should ask yourself before accepting.

- Does it meet your requirements? These can be benefits, commute, hours, etc.
- Is it a good culture fit? Do you feel comfortable interacting with the other therapists on staff?
- Do the pros of the new position outweigh the cons of leaving your current position?
- Does it bring you closer to your professional goals?

If you answered "yes" to all of these questions and feel good about accepting the position, congratulations! You have found a great fit.

WHAT CAN I EXPECT DURING THE FIRST FEW DAYS IN A NEW JOB?

Most employers have an orientation process to get you going the first few days. This orientation experience serves as a tool to ensure you are comfortable in your new role. The level of orientation and training depends on the size of the organization.

Smaller organizations might have a looser or more informal model, while larger organizations will likely be more structured.

During your first days on the job, it's up to you to let your supervisor know what you need. You are responsible for communicating what areas you're struggling in and uncomfortable with as well as what resources you need to do the job to the best of your ability.

Be sure to speak up and don't wait for someone to ask you what you need. Think proactively, based on what you observe, in order to lay a good foundation for success in your new position.

The first few days at any job are all about learning and figuring out the culture of your new workplace.

Career Tree Network

WHAT SHOULD I EXPECT DURING THE ONBOARDING AND ORIENTATION PROCESS?

Once you've officially accepted an offer, you'll begin the onboarding process. During the first few days or weeks at a new position, staff will walk you through all of the details and procedures you need to know in order to best perform in your new role.

As a therapy professional, your employer will (safely) assume that you know proper techniques and general information about your profession. Because of this, the onboarding/orientation process will be specifically targeted to what it's like to work for that employer.

They will give you a tour, discuss workplace policies, and go over documentation systems with you. Rather than focusing on the job duties themselves, employers will typically train you on a secondary level.

WHAT DO EMPLOYERS EXPECT FROM A NEW EMPLOYEE?

At the beginning of an employer-employee relationship, the employers have an open slate and open mind. They expect that the person hired will meet their needs. Ultimately, they expect that the person who arrives on Monday morning will be the same person they selected in the interview, chosen for their skills and characteristics.

Employers expect new employees to live up to all of the elements laid out in the job description, that were discussed in the interview. They expect that employees will meet the qualifications, work the scheduled hours, and provide the care that they promised.

When a new employee shows up and attempts to change their availability, walk back their experiences and qualifications, or change what they said during the interview process, the employer loses confidence in their selection.

Basically it all comes down to one thing: be the person that your employer thought they were hiring.

Career Tree Network

WHAT SHOULD MY PRIORITIES BE GOING INTO MY FIRST DAY IN A NEW POSITION?

CONGRATULATIONS! You've landed a new job. Now what?

Going into your first day, ask yourself: Why did I apply for this opening? What about my previous position led me to take this step?

If you're able to identify what was missing at your previous job, you'll be able to better understand what your priorities should be going into your new one. If there was tension with the upper-level management, focus on creating a healthy relationship with your new management right off the bat. Find out what the expectations are right away.

If you're trying out a new setting, prioritize open-mindedness as you start out. You wanted to change settings to learn more and grow as a therapist… in order to do that, you have to be willing to listen more than you talk.

Whatever it was that brought you to your first day at a new job, make that your top priority.

SOME THINGS THAT ARE IMPORTANT TO DO IN A NEW POSITION:
- Observe the workplace norms
- Create positive relationships with patients and coworkers
- Ask questions if there's any uncertainty
- Learn your place in this already-established professional setting

HOW CAN I IMPRESS MY NEW EMPLOYER DURING THE FIRST FEW DAYS ON THE JOB?

There are some universal rules you should observe at any new position. Show up on time, dress professionally (or within the organization's dress code), and don't rush to leave at the end of the day.

Carry around a notebook and pen to show that you are eager about learning the ins and outs of your new workplace. Ask questions when you have them and observe workplace norms. Show your employer that you are open minded and enthusiastic about what's being shared!

WHAT ARE SOME THINGS I CAN DO MY FIRST WEEK TO START OFF ON THE RIGHT FOOT?

The first week at a new position can be overwhelming, but there are ways to ensure that you start off on the right foot. You want to bring an open mind to your new workplace. Your primary goals for the first week should be observing the other therapists on staff and clearing up any questions you have about the facility.

Be sure to ask questions, observe, and be ready and willing to learn. Your new coworkers and supervisor won't know what you're confused about and what you need if you don't communicate any questions you have.

HOW CAN I STAND OUT IN MY NEW JOB?

In a new position, it's important to stand out. The employer hired you because they like you and believe you can do the job...now show them they made the right decision! Employers want employees who are willing to go the extra mile, help where needed, and deal with the small things too, like refilling the coffee pot or cleaning an extra dish. Though these things aren't expected, employers are impressed by small acts. This is what separates the good employees from the great.

They already have an expectation that you will do your job, but you can go above and beyond to really impress them. Of course, a general enthusiasm about your new position and a positive attitude go a long way too!

Career Tree Network

WHAT IS THE BEST WAY TO EVALUATE MY EMPLOYER'S EXPECTATIONS AGAINST MY OWN?

The best way to compare expectations is to establish clear communication between your superior and yourself. It's important to ask what their expectations are of you and for you to share your expectations with them.

If you feel like your employer's expectations are unrealistic, you need to communicate that. Let them know what your personal expectations are and approach them with an open mind. Typically, if someone has high expectations of you, it's because they see your potential.

It's important to know what is expected of you at your job, and it's also important to be realistic about what you can and cannot do. Setting aside time every few months to speak with your supervisor about your expectations can help clear up any confusion.

I CAN'T FIND MY DREAM POSITION!?! WHAT SHOULD I DO?

Depending on where you are in your career, you'll likely have to compromise on a few things when you land a new position. If you're just starting out, the likelihood that you'll get your dream position in your ideal location with all the compensation you'll ever need is pretty low.

However, as you progress and gain more experience as a therapist, you'll be able to pick and choose your perks a little bit more.

Decide what's most important to you. It's a good idea to have career-related goals that you can reference. Is the position you're in right now going to help you reach that 5-year goal? If yes, maybe it's worth it to stick out that less-than-ideal setting for a little longer. Is your goal to attain a management-level position? To land a job in a certain city?

Would you rather have the higher salary and live in a not-so-desirable area? Or are you willing to take a lower pay rate to be in the city you love? So much of life is a trade-off...especially in the beginning.

Once you've asked yourself what your long-term goals are, you'll be able to see more clearly what's most important today.

WHAT BEHAVIORS WILL HELP ME IN MY NEW POSITION, ESPECIALLY WITH CLIENTS?

Employers want employees who are excited and enthusiastic about the work they're doing. They expect that their employees are reliable, will show up on time, and deliver consistent results.

The best thing you can strive to be in a new position is a sponge. Employers want to see that you are open to learn about the facility, ask questions, and are taking it all in. You'll want to do your best to learn the documentation system, get up to speed on policies and procedures specific to the clinic, and get the administrative stuff done quickly and accurately, so that you're able to make the biggest impact on patients.

Being open, engaged, and willing to learn is important, but it has to be coupled with a sense of rhythm that shows your new employer that you are consistent in your patient care and quality of work.

WHAT HAPPENS DURING A TYPICAL PERFORMANCE REVIEW PROCESS?

Larger organizations tend to have more structured review processes while smaller organizations will likely be less formal about the process. The size of the organization largely dictates what kind of performance review will take place.

Some organizations may have a set worksheet or matrix with a standardized series of criteria in order to evaluate employees on a numeric scale. Some of the categories may include timeliness, communication skills, patient interaction, etc.

Sometimes, these numeric ratings will translate into potential wage increases and other incentives, though not every organization offers raises at the time of the review.

At the most basic level, the goal of any performance review process is to have a discussion around the employee's performance so that the employee and manager can discuss past positive and negative actions, as well as set goals for the future.

HOW DO I RESPOND TO A DISAPPOINTING PERFORMANCE REVIEW?

POOR REVIEWS HAPPEN. Maybe you had a feeling it was coming because you've been off your game lately, or maybe you were blindsided by the disappointing marks. Either way, one bad review does not make or break your career.

Performance reviews exist so that you can become a better therapist. If you got perfect marks every time, there would be no room for growth and no opportunity to reevaluate your methods.

Take time to process your review however you need to, but then engage with your supervisor. Ask questions if you have them, and show them that you have a desire to grow as a therapist.

Come up with a detailed plan that addresses tangible things you can do to improve.

If you believe your review wasn't honest, try to not become defensive. Instead, ask for specific examples of what you did poorly and what you could have done differently.

Career Tree Network

200 WORDS

NETWORKING AND PROFESSIONAL DEVELOPMENT

ESSENTIAL CAREER ADVICE FOR THERAPY PROFESSIONALS

HOW CAN I BUILD MY PROFESSIONAL NETWORK USING SOCIAL MEDIA?

First things first...you need a list of 7-10 organizations where you might like to work. With this targeted list in hand, you can turn to social media to support your networking efforts!

BUILD A LIST OF PEOPLE WHO WORK AT EACH OF YOUR TARGETED ORGANIZATIONS. A good way to build your contact database is to use sites like LinkedIn or Facebook. You can search for employees of your targeted organizations.

Once you find some good contact people, you can reach out to them to share your career search, objective, and sincere interest to come "join the team."

Most organizations use a standard naming convention for employee email addresses. Depending on the organization; an email address for John A. Doe could be:

1. john.doe@domain.com
2. jdoe@domain.com
3. doe.john@domain.com
4. john.a.doe@domain.com

The possibilities are endless, but if you know the convention then you can take an educated guess based on the name of your new contact.

While using social media, you should follow or like each of the companies on your targeted list. You might want to like or comment on their posts to start developing a relationship with the organization and the social media team behind the accounts.

HOW CAN MY SOCIAL MEDIA PROFILES HURT ME DURING THE HIRING PROCESS?

Because we live in a time where everything is online, we live in a time where nothing is off limits. Facebook, LinkedIn, Instagram, Snapchat, Twitter, personal blogs, and any other online presence you've ever had is fair game for employers to scroll through.

Whether or not we like it or agree with it, many employers are searching the dark corners of the internet for you before making a hiring decision.

As a therapist, there's a certain level of professionalism you're expected to meet both online and offline.

THE 3 P'S TO AVOID ON SOCIAL MEDIA:
1. Party pictures.
2. Profanity in excess.
3. Political overkill.

If you're unsure whether your social media accounts are hurting you, take the time to clean up old accounts. Save your crazy college photos to your computer and delete them from your profile, make sure that your posts are set to private, and review old "likes" and "groups" on Facebook. You may be surprised as to what's still there. Also, if you've never Googled yourself, now is the time!

If all else fails, ask a friend to comb through your accounts and check for risky posts.

Career Tree Network

HOW CAN I EFFECTIVELY USE LINKEDIN FOR NETWORKING AND CAREER ADVANCEMENT?

In this day and age, LinkedIn can be your best job-finding friend...if you know how to use it properly. Think of LinkedIn both as a living online resume and as a networking tool.

As your career advances, you can quickly and easily update your profile to reflect new accomplishments, positions, awards, and experiences. Regularly updating your profile shows recruiters and potential employers that you're not stagnant in your career.

Think of LinkedIn as a platform for a mutually beneficial relationship. When you endorse another therapist or write a review of a clinic or staffing agency, they'll be likely to return the favor. With millions of LinkedIn members, it can be tough to stand out. The more endorsements, reviews, and connections you have, the more professional and credible you look to the online world.

Take advantage of the ease of online networking. If a second or third connection on LinkedIn has several mutual connections, consider connecting with them to boost your profile. Remember, every connection you make has the potential to open doors down the road.

That's what networking is all about!

WHAT'S THE BEST WAY TO NETWORK WITH POTENTIAL EMPLOYERS?

In areas with a surplus of therapy professionals, many well qualified candidates struggle to find a new position. Building your professional network is a great avenue to increase your chances of landing a great job.

The first step is to identify 7-10 organizations where you might like to work. You can do this via your knowledge of the area, on-line searches, or from talking to other therapists about potential employers.

With the target organizations identified, the real work can begin. Cold calling is painful and most people avoid it like the plague, but it's an important step in the process.

The plan is to call each of your targeted employers and attempt to speak with a member of Human Resources. Your voice mail or telephone pitch might go something like this:

"Hi, my name is _____ and I'd really like to join your team as a _____. I just wanted to introduce myself and I'd like to see if I can send you my resume to keep on file for open career opportunities down the road."

If possible, obtain an email address and direct phone number for your contact person.

Congratulations, you've laid the foundation for a successful career search!

SHOULD I JOIN MY STATE PROFESSIONAL ASSOCIATION?

YES. There are a variety of reasons, but we'll focus on the potential benefit that joining a professional association can have to your career growth.

Joining professional associations and attending meetings / conferences is an excellent way to interact (and build relationships) with people who may be able to help you achieve your career objectives.

When you attend events, be sure to dress appropriately and bring copies of your business card.

Be quick to extend a smile and handshake to everyone you meet.

It's a little awkward (and unnecessary) to hand out your resume at these events...a business card is more appropriate and much easier to carry. If you don't already have cards printed, you can use an online printer to create a professional business card.

You'll also want to work on your elevator pitch so that the people you meet can quickly learn about you and gain some perspective on your career goals.

WHY SHOULD A THERAPIST JOIN AND GET INVOLVED WITHIN THEIR PROFESSIONAL ASSOCIATION?

You should join your professional association because, as a therapist, you have a profession, not just a job. You don't go to work, complete your tasks, and leave it all behind; you are part of a profession. With that comes a sense of community as well as duty.

Your professional association advocates for the profession on a continual basis. These efforts address payment, marketing, and legislative issues. Without their efforts, the profession could rapidly lose its scope of practice and place.

Extra benefits of membership include great educational opportunities at local, state, and national conferences as well as networking opportunities. Within your association, you will meet other therapists that share your passions; you will find friends and mentors that last a lifetime.

NETWORKING WITH PHYSICIANS AND REFERRAL SOURCES IS A BIT UNCOMFORTABLE FOR ME. ANY SUGGESTIONS?

The most important thing to remember when speaking with referral sources is that you have something in common: you both have the best interest of the patient in mind.

Be sure to communicate that you want the best for your patients and how your skills and services can help meet their organization's goals for its patients.

While it's normal to be intimidated initially, remembering that everyone is on the same page with the same goal in mind can help to calm your nerves.

I'M ATTENDING AN EVENT NEXT WEEK FOR MY PROFESSIONAL ASSOCIATION, WHAT SHOULD I DO TO HELP PREPARE ME FOR NETWORKING?

For any networking event, it would be helpful if you had business cards with you. That way, when you meet people you can easily exchange contact information. Even if it's just a simple, professional-looking card that you print up on your own, it can go a long way to ensure that you're able to keep in touch with the people that you meet. All your card needs to include is your name and email address.

The whole point of networking is meeting people who you can later reach out to for help if you need to. The most important factor is that you're able to reach each other.

It can also be beneficial to obtain a list of attendees, or at least to have some idea of who will be attending. Then, you can think about what questions and topics you might bring up with those people to help fuel the conversation.

Have a goal in mind about what you want to get and who you want to get it from, so that you're not at a loss for questions when the time comes for the event.

Career Tree Network

WHAT ARE SOME TIPS FOR TALKING TO SOMEONE AT A NETWORKING EVENT WITHOUT COMING ACROSS AS OVEREAGER OR PUSHY?

When networking, it's important to try to relate to the person as an individual. Oftentimes, people try to bypass the friendship-building part of a relationship and attempt to talk business right off the bat. While there is definitely a professional element to the relationship, you want to try to be personal as your first step.

The business side will come later, and often it will come naturally.

By leading into a potential networking opportunity socially, with a friendship in mind, you will be more relaxed and ultimately more effective down the road.

It's okay to ask someone questions about where they live, their family, and hobbies before getting down to business about how the two of you might mutually benefit one another in a professional relationship down the road.

Remember, people want to help their friends.

WHAT ARE SOME AVENUES TO BECOME MORE ACTIVE WITHIN A PROFESSIONAL ASSOCIATION?

If you are hoping to get more involved in a professional association, first determine what aspects of the association interest you.

Once you know what you are interested in getting more involved in, peruse the association's newsletters and websites for information. Then contact the Executive Director or anyone else within the organization who is involved. A simple way to start is by attending a conference, a district meeting and / or a board meeting.

The board is always willing to help members find activities that interest them.

HOW DO YOU OBTAIN A LEADERSHIP POSITION WITHIN YOUR PROFESSIONAL ASSOCIATION?

Start by joining a committee that plans events or handles a certain aspect of the association's activities. After attending meetings and becoming more aware of the avenues within the association, opportunities for leadership positions will arise.

Find mentors along the way that will help guide and support you as you step into new roles.

HOW WILL BEING INVOLVED IN YOUR PROFESSIONAL ASSOCIATION BENEFIT YOUR CAREER?

Involvement in professional associations can be crucial to your career. They connect you with mentors who can inspire and help you to advance your professional skills. The networking opportunities available in associations can also result in offers to teach or practice in new geographic areas as well as new settings and environments.

WHAT ARE SOME GOOD RESOURCES TO TAKE ADVANTAGE OF THAT WILL HELP ME ADVANCE MY CAREER?

As you look to advance your career, one of the best things you can do is actively look for opportunities to increase your responsibility. Even if you're relatively happy in your current position at the moment, taking on additional responsibility can open doors for you down the road.

It's also a great idea to look into additional continuing education opportunities. Employers are impressed by people who are consistently looking to improve their skills as a therapist. On the same note, pursuing different certifications can set you apart.

Basically, anything you do to step up and help out above your mandatory work tasks is going to help you in the long run. Volunteer, take on different roles, and utilize your professional association as a networking opportunity.

WHAT ARE SOME TIPS FOR SETTING PROFESSIONAL GOALS?

One of the best things you can do for your career is to set and commit to professional goals. It's important to have long-term goals and to create short-term goals that will help you accomplish those bigger, broader achievements down the road.

When setting your career-related goals, be sure that they are quantifiable. For example, if one of your goals is to become a Director of Rehab, then a series of measurable short-term goals could be to volunteer for additional responsibilities and then obtain a managerial position.

Your goals also need to be realistic. You want to hit that sweet spot that is both challenging and attainable. Remember, it's always an option to reconsider and edit your goals as your career progresses.

WHY IS IT IMPORTANT TO SET GOALS IN THIS PROFESSION?

As a therapy professional, you spend much of your time dedicated to your profession. It's because of the time you dedicate that you really owe it to yourself and your patients to be the best therapist you can be.

Your patients deserve the best care, the most cutting-edge treatment methods, and the most effective care available. As a therapist, it's important that you take steps to constantly improve your skills and push yourself forward, so that you can provide optimal patient care. That's why goal setting is important.

By having goals and achieving milestones in your practice, you get to one day become the therapist that people refer their family members to; you get to be a person who greatly impacts their patients' lives.

If you're not setting goals and you're stagnant within your position, you're not working in your best interest or the best interest of the patients. Goals allow you to see those opportunities for growth and service.

WHAT ARE SOME SAMPLE CAREER GOALS THAT THERAPY PROFESSIONALS MIGHT HAVE ON THEIR RADAR?

A great trend right now, especially within Physical Therapy, is to complete the doctorate program. This is an example of a great, solid, attainable, and quantifiable goal.

Additional goals would include getting certified within a specialty area, completing a residency, becoming a department manager, becoming a Director of Rehab, doing consulting, or breaking into some other niche setting. Niche settings can be working with a certain population, such as neuro patients, or working for a specific employer that you respect and admire.

IF I'VE BEEN AT MY CURRENT POSITION FOR A LONG TIME AND HAVE NO INTENTION OF CHANGING JOBS, WHAT CAN I DO TO CONTINUE LEARNING AND NOT GROW STAGNANT WITHIN MY POSITION?

At the end of the day, it's your job as the employee to be in charge of your own professional development. Employers may offer opportunities such as training and special projects from time to time, but really it's the therapist's job to actively seek out those additional opportunities.

If you have interest in developing your skill set within a certain practice area or specialization, you should look for those opportunities, then bring up your ideas to your employer, and ask for support. Employers ultimately want what is best for the clinic, so it's likely that they'll be on board.

It takes your individual initiative to continue learning within a long-term position because employers are often too busy to think about people's individual aspirations and opportunities.

WHAT OPPORTUNITIES SHOULD I SEEK OUT FOR SKILL DEVELOPMENT?

There are many opportunities within the therapy disciplines to pursue continuing education. Whether online or in person, engaging in these additional training programs can only positively impact your skill set and your career.

When deciding which courses to take, it's important to think of continuing education opportunities as a vehicle by which you can actually open new doors. Don't just take courses that fit nicely into your schedule or look like an easy way to fill some requirements... choose courses that might actually benefit your career, challenge you to learn, interest you, and complement your patient population.

WHAT IS SOME ADVICE FOR EFFECTIVE COLLABORATION WITH OTHER THERAPISTS IN THE DEPARTMENT?

Think of collaboration as an opportunity to create a positive environment within the therapy department. The best way to create a collaborative department is to use your colleagues as resources for your own development as a therapist. You can also honor them by talking up their expertise with your caseload. If you do this, and your patients end up on their schedule at any point, you and your colleague will build a sense of trust and confidence.

Another beneficial practice is to bring your colleagues into your treatment sessions. If you ever have questions about a patient's progress, or even if you just want a second set of eyes, your coworkers are there as resources.

WHAT STEPS SHOULD I TAKE TO BUILD MY REPUTATION AS A TOP-QUALITY THERAPY PROFESSIONAL?

There are a lot of certifications available within the different therapy disciplines. Employers often look favorably upon candidates who have those certifications and additional training/education.

The most important factor when attempting to build your reputation is to show that you're not just going through the motions, but that you care about the quality of therapy you provide and are committed to it. It's also important to be active within your professional associations.

Employers want to see therapists who have gone above and beyond what is required of them. It shows that you're dedicated to the field. It shows them that you don't just show up and do your job at base value, but that you're proactive, passionate, and qualified.

WHAT ARE SOME UNDER-UTILIZED JOB SEARCH TIPS THAT CAN BE ESPECIALLY EFFECTIVE FOR A THERAPY PROFESSIONAL?

While the idea of networking can be daunting for some people, it can actually be the best job search tool. A common mistake that many people make is only searching for and applying to positions that are posted online. Often, though, open positions never get posted because they're quickly filled through connections to the organization.

In an environment where many organizations don't do much to advertise their openings, the best way to learn is to be proactive in your search and network.

Unfortunately, the job you want and have applied for may be filled by someone else who had already networked with the clinic and made his or her interest known before you ever even clicked submit.

It's a common misconception that every opening will be posted online. However, because the job you want might never make it to that stage, it's important to show employers that you are active and interested.

200 WORDS

JOB
RELOCATION

ESSENTIAL CAREER ADVICE FOR THERAPY PROFESSIONALS

THERE ARE LOTS OF PT OPENINGS IN MY LOCAL AREA. WHY SHOULD I CONSIDER RELOCATING FOR A POSITION?

"You cannot always wait for the perfect time; sometimes you must dare to jump." — Unknown

Starting a new life with a new job in a new city can be scary. In fact, sometimes we get so scared thinking about it that we close our minds to the possibility entirely. But it can also be the best thing we ever do. There are endless opportunities waiting for us outside the confines of our current zip code!

As a therapy professional, your skills are in high demand. Sometimes a change of scenery is a great way to not only fall in love with a new community, but also to gain valuable experience at a new organization.

Often, we cling to what we know and don't consider that something new might shift our lives in a good direction. In many parts of the US, therapy professionals are in very high demand.

For people who are location flexible and willing to try a new geographic area, you can be sure that your skills will be very well rewarded and you'll also be serving a community to ensure that therapy is more readily available to people in need.

IF I KNOW I WANT TO RELOCATE, WHAT IS A GOOD TIMELINE TO BEGIN LOOKING FOR JOBS?

If you've got your heart set on making a move, you can start looking for jobs as early as possible. Relocation can take a long time; one of the most time-consuming factors is setting up a new position.

Even if you're not ready to start applying right away, it's never to early to build a network. The people that you connect with via LinkedIn and various professional associations can potentially help out when it's time to make the move.

In many cases, employers are willing to hold the position for the right candidate. You can put some feelers out and start applying for openings to see who is willing to hold the position until you move. It doesn't hurt to get started as soon as possible!

Career Tree Network

IF I'VE NEVER VISITED THE EMPLOYER BECAUSE IT'S IN A DIFFERENT CITY OR STATE, HOW CAN I BE SURE IT'S A GOOD FIT?

CONGRATULATIONS! YOU'RE THINKING OF RELOCATING.

Moving to a new city or state is scary and thrilling all at the same time. Starting a new job, especially when you've never spent time at the facility, can be just as scary.

If you can, make a trip to the potential workplace. Use up the last of that PTO and take a long weekend to your possible new home. Set up an in-person interview, ask to meet with other employees, and take the time to tour both the workplace and the surrounding area.

Bring a checklist of things that are important to you and focus on those items. Even by spending a few hours visualizing yourself at work and at home in this new setting, you'll likely get a gut feeling whether it would be a good fit or not.

Unfortunately, it's not always possible to visit a place before making a commitment. In that case, take advantage of the internet! Many facilities have online photos, virtual tours, and videos about their services. You can also connect with current employees to learn about workplace morale and culture to determine whether it will be a good fit.

SHOULD I EXPECT RELOCATION COMPENSATION FROM MY NEW EMPLOYER?

It really depends on whether the position you want is difficult to fill. If there are plenty of local candidates interested in an opening, it's not likely that you'll receive a relocation bonus. However, depending on the location and practice setting, there may not be many local candidates available or interested. In this case, as with higher level managerial positions, the employer will often be willing to negotiate additional compensation to cover your move.

Because an employer isn't willing to pay for your moving expenses, doesn't mean that they aren't willing to hold a position for you. You'll have to make the move on your own dime.

If you're willing to cover your own relocation expenses, it can help to include that information in your cover letter, so that the employer knows that you don't require relocation compensation.

You might also want to remove your mailing address from your resume so that you appear as a local candidate. This will at least get you in the running and give you the opportunity to explain that you are moving soon.

200 WORDS

EXPLORING JOBS OUTSIDE OF YOUR IDEAL PRACTICE SETTING

ESSENTIAL CAREER ADVICE FOR THERAPY PROFESSIONALS

WHAT IS THE BENEFIT IN TAKING A JOB OUTSIDE OF MY IDEAL PRACTICE SETTING?

Often, therapy professionals have preconceived notions about certain practice settings and even though they haven't tried them personally, they automatically discount them. For example, Home Health is a practice setting that some Physical Therapists avoid...but then after doing a job shadow or giving it a try, most find it very rewarding in terms of autonomy of care and flexibility.

When therapists step into a new setting with an open mind, they often find that the setting has many benefits they wouldn't have realized had they not been willing to try it out. Each practice has both drawbacks and benefits, but there's no way to know what's best for you if you rule out a certain setting.

On an even larger scale, as a therapy professional, society is very much in need of your skills. That includes individuals in every age, income bracket, geographic location and background. By closing your mind to certain communities, there's a vast majority of the population that gets left behind.

Most employers will gladly allow you to perform a job shadow within their setting. This might be a good place to start if you're open to explore.

WHAT IS THE BENEFIT TO EXPLORE OTHER POSITIONS IF I'M RELATIVELY HAPPY IN MY CURRENT ROLE?

If you're secure in your position, you don't have much to lose by exploring other opportunities. There are likely positions out there that you don't even know about that can offer you a higher salary, better benefits, or more flexible hours.

It's great that you're relatively happy in your current position. But remember: the marketplace is in high demand of your skills as a therapist. Your employer is maximizing what they charge patients for your service, so from an economic perspective, you also should look at maximizing what you earn.

There is always a benefit to seeing what else is available, so that you are confident you are being compensated fairly.

Many employers struggle to fill positions, so it never hurts to see what else is out there. An employer who's struggling to fill a role will typically be very agreeable in terms of salary and benefits.

Career Tree Network

200 WORDS

ADVICE AND PERSPECTIVES FROM THERAPY PROFESSIONALS WHO WORK IN ACADEMICS

ESSENTIAL CAREER ADVICE FOR THERAPY PROFESSIONALS

WHAT ADVICE DO YOU HAVE FOR SOMEONE INTERESTED IN WORKING WITHIN ACADEMICS?

Most college faculty positions have three components which include research, teaching, and service. First, you will need to decide if you want to be a researcher. If you choose to be a researcher, then look to obtain your PhD. If you are more interested in the clinical side, look to obtain some professional certifications and an advanced degree – Clinical Doctorate. Good college faculty are passionate and eager to share their knowledge and help students.

Academia offers the chance for a therapy practitioner to have a larger effect on our practice by instilling a strong foundation of love for the practice in others. Currently, there is a shortage of academic faculty nationwide. Stay connected with practice and research in order to continue to improve and shape academic and practical programs.

WHY WOULD SOMEONE DECIDE TO BECOME A PROFESSOR OR COLLEGE FACULTY MEMBER?

After gaining experience working in your clinic, you may be asked to train new employees or lead workshops in clinical education to help others enhance their skills. If you are asked to do so, you will find that the people you teach are generally energized and passionate about what they are learning.

Small teaching experiences like these may lead you into seeking larger teaching opportunities with more demands and less experienced learners.

When thinking about stepping into an academic setting, consider the current changes and challenges, positive and negative, of all of your career options. Find out what successes and failures practitioners, professors, and managers are seeing due to changes in the industry.

Find out how you can be most useful in your practice to both support clinical learning, and also navigate the changing healthcare arena. Academia may allow you to do both.

Career Tree Network

WHAT IS SOMETHING THAT MOST PEOPLE DON'T REALIZE ABOUT WORKING AS A PROFESSOR OR COLLEGE FACULTY MEMBER?

There are great opportunities for learning within a college environment. It's fun learning from all types of people who are part of the campus community. It's a stimulating work environment dedicated to consistent improvement and growth.

Most people don't realize that many college faculty members work long hours...an average of around 60 hours per week.

Part of being an academic is understanding that all knowledge leads to more questions. Seeking new knowledge and understanding is a constant state.

WHAT ARE THE GREATEST CHALLENGES THAT SOMEONE MIGHT FACE IN ACADEMICS?

Due to the long working hours and bulk of work, it can be challenging to complete all of your responsibilities and complete them with good quality.

While rewarding, working in academics is a very different pace than working in direct patient care. It can take a while to gain comfort within an academic role, but as with all positions, things tend to become more clear with time and experience.

WHAT IS MOST ENJOYABLE ABOUT BEING A PROFESSOR OR COLLEGE FACULTY MEMBER?

The ability to share your passion for therapy with your students is the most enjoyable aspect of teaching. The passionate environment is energetic and exciting, and it fosters positive growth in individuals as well as in the industry. You also get to help people learn and grow as they transition from students to working therapists. You play a huge roll in shaping people's lives as they learn the skills necessary for lifelong careers.

WHAT DO YOU LEAST ENJOY ABOUT BEING A PROFESSOR OR COLLEGE FACULTY MEMBER?

Due to changing health trends, therapists are in very high demand in terms of wellness, prevention, productive aging, living community consultation, and health management for an aging population. With this increase in need, universities are accepting more students and programs into therapy disciplines, and as professors, it is difficult to meet the demands of all of the students. Due to the imbalance of students to professors, there are not enough hours in the day to prepare students as well as we have in the past. Students will need to be prepared to learn on the fly and soak up as much information as possible—and quickly—especially once they begin their first jobs.

Another challenge to professions in academia is the organizational politics that can sometimes interfere with the mission to educate. Management changes are difficult to navigate as faculty need to keep focused on the students rather than jockeying for power and control.

FROM AN ACADEMIC FOCUSED STANDPOINT, WHAT TRENDS ARE YOU SEEING IN THE PROFESSION?

The most current trend in the therapy profession is reestablishing its role in mental health. With the opioid epidemic and with numbers of those living with anxiety and PTSD, there is a need to regain a foothold in the area of mental health. This is where the profession began.

More and more therapy professionals are marketing themselves in to niches to better serve a small group of patients. This is a good strategy, and allows professionals to become experts in specific areas of therapy.

One concern that many therapists see, is regarding reimbursement and the ability for the healthcare system of tomorrow to continue to support paying the high cost of service.

FROM AN ACADEMIC FOCUSED STANDPOINT, HOW HAS THE PROFESSION CHANGED IN THE LAST 20 YEARS?

During the last 20 years, the profession has worked very hard to claim and validate its identity. This was done through research, science and advocacy. Therapists developed the Practice Framework that clearly identifies the domain and process of OT. Since the creation of a universal language for OT, research and advocacy have been more focused. In addition, evidenced-based care, client-centered care and adjusting to the changes in health care have contributed to a more outcomes-focused therapy system.

Student loans and the cost of education have increased drastically. This burden affects many students long after graduation.

With so many intelligent researchers who have dedicated their lives to the advance of therapy, the field will only grow and strengthen in the next 20 years.

200 WORDS

TRAVEL POSITIONS

ESSENTIAL CAREER ADVICE FOR THERAPY PROFESSIONALS

WHAT IS IT LIKE TO WORK AS A TRAVEL THERAPIST?

Because the majority of contracts (SNFs in particular) have high productivity standards—usually at 90%—you have to be organized and confident in your position and your skills. The days are fast-paced and you learn how to be as quick as possible in learning the new physical location of your setting, as well as in completing your documentation on a potentially new EMR or paper system. All travel contracts are paid by the hour, so when you clock out at the end of your shift, you are able to leave your work at the office, and you do not have to work overtime unless you agree to it in advance. Since you are expected to reach 90% productivity, you must make your needs known to reach that expectation (i.e. making sure your computer or iPad is not shared with other staff members).

Overall, working as a travel therapist is very rewarding. You learn a lot, and although it can be stressful to learn the workings of a new clinic and hit the ground running, it usually only takes a week to acclimate. You must be flexible, adaptable, and able to handle adversity. The benefits far outweigh the potential for stress.

WHAT'S THE BEST WAY TO LEARN ABOUT A TRAVEL POSITION AND WHETHER OR NOT IT IS A GOOD OPPORTUNITY?

It's a great idea to reach out to another therapist you know who has travel experience. If you don't know any traveling therapists, the internet has many great resources including FAQ and blogs about travel therapy. Signing up for private emails from traveling companies also tends to be a good way to learn what's currently out there.

The best thing you can do is establish a relationship with a recruiter you like and trust. Instead of wasting time searching online for leads on contracts that may not work out, spend your free time taking advantage of the benefits and adventures of travel.

With each new contract, your focus should be on what benefits they provide, and how they can accommodate your wants and needs. You have the power to say no to bad opportunities, and keep looking for better ones that suit your needs.

WHY DID YOU INITIALLY DECIDE TO WORK AS A TRAVEL THERAPIST?

Travel therapy positions allow you to explore your career options before committing to a city, state, or job setting. If you are unsure of what type of practice you would like to work for, you have the opportunity to experience many types. A huge benefit of traveling, is that if you don't like one contract, you don't have to worry about being tied down to it for a long period of time.

Traveling allows you to learn more about the industry before making a full-time decision, offers good compensation, and gives you the opportunity to travel to different states.

WHAT SHOULD YOU KNOW ABOUT TRAVELING BEFORE YOU GET STARTED?

Working as a travel therapist is a continuous learning process. It's comforting to know that you are never tied down to a bad situation for long. If you aren't happy you have the ability to move on and get to a better situation. Don't settle for less than what you expect for your own happiness. There are many opportunities for you out there to explore and experience.

One thing you should know about travel positions is that not all contracts are 13 weeks. Unless it's in the contract, the lengths are not set in stone. Guaranteed weekly hours do not mean guaranteed length of contract. If the situation is not working well, there is always an out for both parties, and either party can cancel the contract with fair notice as set in the contract.

Companies are not afraid to use this notice to suit their needs, so don't be afraid to use it to suit yours. If you are in a "settling contract" and a better opportunity comes along, don't limit your career. You should have your recruiter working to find you the best opportunities even when you are currently on contract, especially if you aren't fulfilled in your current situation.

WHAT ARE SOME OF THE BENEFITS TO WORKING AS A TRAVEL THERAPIST?

The financial benefits of a travel contract are enticing. There are weekly direct deposits, tax-free per diems for housing and meals, low cost medial insurance, vision and dental insurance, life insurance, short term and long term disability insurance, free malpractice coverage, reimbursement of licensure fees, moving fees, CEUs and 401K plans. You will find financial security in working as a travel therapist, and if you have student debt, you will begin to quickly pay it off.

Aside from the compensation, some other huge benefits to traveling are the ability to experience living in different parts of the country, the flexibility, and the opportunity to work in various settings and learn from a lot of different therapists.

WHAT ARE SOME OF THE DRAWBACKS TO WORKING AS A TRAVEL THERAPIST?

When you aren't on contract you don't get paid. You can lose your health benefits if you don't sign up for COBRA or pay for your own individual medical insurance. Yes, there will always be available contracts, but if you are particular about a specific setting or location, you need to prepare yourself for the potential weeks or months of not working.

When it comes to filing taxes, things can get more complicated because you have to file tax returns for each state you've worked.

WHAT ARE THE MOST ENJOYABLE ASPECTS OF BEING A TRAVELER?

There are several benefits to travel therapy contracts. If you love to see new areas of the country, meet new people, and learn new things at each assignment, you will enjoy the opportunity. The increased income can also help you get student loans paid off quicker and help you start saving for your future.

You will also enjoy growing and expanding your skills as a physical therapist. Right after graduation, there are so many aspects of the workforce that are unknown. You will learn what "good" benefits are, how to manage productivity standards, how to use EMR systems, and how to talk to patients and other medical professionals with confidence. There are so many aspects of this career that are not taught in school or clinical rotations, but working as a traveler provides the time and experience to test the waters of different settings, treat patient populations you may have never been exposed to, and most importantly figure out your preferences.

WHAT ARE THE LEAST ENJOYABLE ASPECTS OF BEING A TRAVELER?

The most frustrating aspect of travel therapy is when you find a contract in your preferred setting or location, but you have to wait for an opening to come up. It's a game of supply and demand, and sometimes the supply just isn't available at the time you want it. You have to adapt and learn to settle on some contracts if you want to stay busy.

Another difficult part of traveling is the fact that you may miss out on certain activities or holidays back home. The benefits and downfalls are all trade-offs, but in the end the benefits of traveling usually make up for what you miss. You will have to make some sacrifices, but you can usually work out the most important things that you need to be back home for.

WHAT ARE THE GREATEST CHALLENGES OF BEING A TRAVELER?

If you start as a traveler right after school, some of your greatest challenges may be managing the level of responsibility that you get thrown into. It is possible (and likely) that you will be the only physical therapist in your setting and you will manage assistants and departments you may never have worked in before. If you don't have a mentor to turn to for questions, you will have to figure things out on your own and make tough decisions. In facing all of these challenging situations, you will grow more confident in your knowledge and skills in front of patients and colleagues.

Another challenge of traveling is if you get your hopes on working at a particular location, and in the end, the contract doesn't work out. You must be flexible to some degree and not narrow your demands too much.

WHAT ADVICE DO YOU HAVE FOR SOMEONE INTERESTED IN TRAVEL POSITIONS?

Take your time to talk to, and ask questions of several recruiters to find the right fit for you. Find someone who will be available and honest while working to meet your needs.

If you are uncomfortable with your recruiter for any reason, you always have the opportunity to switch and work with another company or recruiter. If you find multiple recruiters that you enjoy working with, you then have extra help in looking for your next assignment which allows more variety. If you are looking for a certain location, setting, or pay rate, having more than one recruiter working for you allows you the best opportunity to find what you are looking for.

Every contract you take is going to be different, which means you have to be willing to dive head first into a company's culture that has already been established. You are the chameleon of the therapy profession when deciding to be a traveling therapist, so you have to be willing to adapt.

Career Tree Network

WHAT IS SOMETHING THAT MOST PEOPLE DON'T REALIZE ABOUT WORKING IN A TRAVEL POSITION?

You don't get paid sick days or vacation days in this line of work. However, that doesn't mean you can't go on a vacation you've had planned, or call in sick for that matter. You simply need to build in your days off at the beginning of your contract, or contact your supervisor as soon as you know you can't come in to work. You won't get your hourly rate or your per diem for the time missed, but if you are working as a traveler year round, life is going to happen and you have to accept that some days you won't get paid. Your contract will usually have a clause in it discussing the change in your paycheck if you miss part, or all, of a workday.

Another thing that many people don't realize is that a lot of times, since you are filling a temporary need, you are offered extensions or even permanent placements. If you fall into a contract that you really love, you can usually negotiate a permanent position at that clinic.

Career Tree Network

200 WORDS

MENTORS AND MENTEES

ESSENTIAL CAREER ADVICE FOR THERAPY PROFESSIONALS

WHAT IS THE BENEFIT OF HAVING A PROFESSIONAL MENTOR? IS IT WORTH IT?

Only good can come from a mentor/mentee relationship. A mentor will help you navigate your current position while also setting you up for success down the road.

A mentor can relate to you and understand your career goals. They can help inspire you to achieve those goals. From a therapy perspective, a mentor can help ensure that you're growing in your skills. They can provide you with access to and knowledge of current treatment methods to help broaden your scope.

Mentor/mentee relationships are great tools to advance your career as a therapist.

HOW DO I GO ABOUT SEEKING A MENTOR?

Establishing a relationship with a mentor is a great investment in your career. Some larger organizations will have official mentorship programs that will automatically assign you a mentor. Within smaller organizations, it's typically your responsibility to find someone either in the company or externally in the profession who you look up to and may benefit from.

In both cases, once a mentor has been assigned, the level of engagement is really up to you as the mentee. It's important that you make your needs and desires known to your mentor, so that they can be of the most help to you.

Most therapists are willing to engage in a mentor/mentee relationship. Approach someone who you think would be a good fit and ask if they're willing to help you in any capacity.

HOW CAN I MAKE THE MOST OUT OF A MENTOR AND MENTEE RELATIONSHIP?

In a mentor/mentee relationship, you really get out of it what you put into it. It's important to have regular meetings scheduled with your mentor; it can even be something as simple as grabbing coffee together.

At the beginning of your relationship, identify and communicate specific skills and techniques that you're hoping to learn. As you continue to meet, your mentor can keep his or her ears open for what you're looking for.

The weight of the relationship is primarily in your hands as the mentee; it's up to you to drive. The mentor can't know what you're looking to get out of it you don't effectively and regularly communicate. They can't help you if they don't know what you need help with!

Career Tree Network

200 WORDS

PROMOTIONS

ESSENTIAL CAREER ADVICE FOR THERAPY PROFESSIONALS

WHAT CAN A THERAPY PROFESSIONAL DO TO SET THEMSELVES APART WITHIN THE FIELD?

As a therapist, you are in the business of people. Often we get caught up in treatment plans and paperwork, but the most important thing you can do as a therapist is to take a step back and really get to know your patients.

The most effective therapists are the ones who have a vested interest in their patients' recovery. Find a population and practice setting that allows your compassion and interpersonal relationships to flourish, and you will certainly find success.

HOW CAN I COMPETE FOR JOB OPPORTUNITIES WITH THERAPISTS WHO ARE MORE EXPERIENCED?

As a recent grad, it might feel like you're often losing out on positions to therapy professionals with more experience. And, while many employers do prefer to hire folks with more experience, there are several characteristics that newer grads have that can be just as attractive.

HERE ARE SOME EXAMPLES:
1. Newer grads have access to the latest and greatest practice techniques, theories, and research.
2. Newer grads tend to be more flexible. Older therapists can become somewhat set in their ways and also often have scheduling limitations. If you are flexible and willing to help as needed, be sure to use this as a strong selling point.
3. Recent grads have passion and excitement to start their career and make an impact. Be sure to communicate how this will translate into quality patient care and a solid work ethic.

At the end of the day there are many reasons why employers often prefer to hire newer grads for their open therapy positions. Your strategy within the hiring process should be to emphasize why you are uniquely qualified to fill the open position.

WHAT SEPARATES TOP THERAPY PROFESSIONALS FROM AVERAGE ONES?

Rehab managers look to hire the best and brightest therapy professionals to fill their open positions. Employers want a therapist who strives for excellence, has a passion for continual improvement / learning, and makes patient care their priority.

STRIVE FOR EXCELLENCE
Look for ways to be the best at what you do. Take pride. Do good work.

PASSION FOR CONTINUAL IMPROVEMENT AND LEARNING
Develop an eagerness for continuing education. Make keeping your license current more than a necessity, and think of it as an opportunity for personal growth to expand your skills. Look for mentors who can help you. Offer to be a mentor to another therapist.

PATIENT CARE IS TOP PRIORITY
The biggest thing that makes a therapist great is genuine patient care. Therapists who advocate for their patients make a lasting impact. Top therapists are willing to take risks in order to provide better care. They are unafraid to speak up on behalf of the patient. Top therapists listen with intention and interpret what's being communicated to them. They take the time to know the patient and their family because they care about the outcome of their services.

200 WORDS

ADVICE AND PERSPECTIVES FROM THERAPISTS IN LEADERSHIP POSITIONS

ESSENTIAL CAREER ADVICE FOR THERAPY PROFESSIONALS

WHAT DO EMPLOYERS EXPECT FROM A REHAB MANAGER?

Employers expect that a Rehab Manager is business-minded. They're looking to see that you're driving revenue, that your utilization of resources is high, and that the clinical outcomes are excellent.

As a Rehab Manager, much of the success of the clinic falls on your shoulders. When the clinic is seeing poor results, it's likely that your employer will look to you to change and improve the outcome. Your employer expects managers to take responsibility for their leadership.

WHAT IS A REHAB MANAGER'S MAIN RESPONSIBILITY?

MEETINGS, MEETINGS, MEETINGS!

As a Rehab Manager, you are expected to be in department meetings, administrative meetings, and family care meetings. A lot of the role revolves around communication and relaying messages from one person or department to another.

Rehab Managers are always loaded with appointments, so good time management and communication skills are essential to success.

WHAT IS ONE ASPECT OF BEING A REHAB MANAGER THAT MOST PEOPLE DON'T REALIZE?

At any given moment, a Rehab Manager is pulled into ten different directions. There is a constant laundry list of things that you have to get done. It's a never-ending barrage of to-do lists.

Sometimes, it can be difficult to stay positive and excited when there are so many responsibilities. There's definitely a large degree of stress involved in being a Rehab Manager that many people tend to overlook.

Rehab Managers take on a vast quantity of work and often have to take work home.

WHAT MAKES A GOOD REHAB MANAGER?

The best Rehab Managers understand both the patient-focused clinical aspect as well as the business side. Any therapist at management level will have the clinical experience necessary to manage, but not everyone understands the business part of the equation. You have to be willing to drive the business into success.

In addition to understanding the two sides of the clinic, managers also have to stay on top of staff to ensure that things get done in a timely manner. Rehab Managers are proactive in leading.

Well-rounded Rehab Managers ensure that clinical skills and patient care are excellent in order to generate revenue for the business.

WHAT MAKES FOR A POOR OR INEFFECTIVE REHAB MANAGER?

Inflexibility is the worst attribute in a Rehab Manager. As a manager, you have to be willing to roll with the changes and bend your personal opinions and priorities in the best interests of the clinic.

You also have to be able to handle a fast-paced and ever-changing schedule. Managers who are unable to jump from one thing to another will have a difficult time keeping their heads above water.

It's also important maintain a calm composure when faced with a million challenges at once. If you're flexible, quick on your feet, and willing to roll with the punches, you will probably be a successful manager.

WHAT IS THE MOST ENJOYABLE ASPECT OF WORKING AS A REHAB MANAGER?

If you love working with people, the ability to foster and build teamwork with people who are passionate about what they do is very rewarding. It is gratifying to be a trusted source and to help your staff with questions or challenges. You are someone that others can learn from.

Therapists are most effective when they feel that they are valued and appreciated. As a manager, you will play a large role in helping others feel valued and growing their passions.

When you are successful in creating an environment of respect and trust, you will create a team that works hard towards finding the best clinical outcomes for your patients, therefore creating a successful and growing business.

WHAT IS THE LEAST ENJOYABLE ASPECT OF WORKING AS A REHAB MANAGER?

One of the least enjoyable aspects as Rehab Manager is to meet the expectations set by the clinic's administration. Since the upper level management does not always see the therapists working in their daily roles, it can fall on the Rehab Manager to find middle ground between expectations of therapists and administrators.

Another challenge is the number of hours a Rehab Manager works. The job is never limited to 40 hours per week, and often times you have to take work home. There is always a possibility for burnout within the role, but you have to stay positive.

WHAT ARE THE GREATEST CHALLENGES THAT REHAB MANAGERS FACE?

Ever-changing regulations with Medicare and healthcare are constant challenges for Rehab Managers. There are so many types of insurances that dictate the level of care that clinics can provide.

In past years, you might be able to treat patients for longer periods of time or co-treat, but now insurance systems are less generous and limit how much care you are able to provide.

WHAT ARE THE BEST STEPS TO TAKE TO PREPARE FOR A MANAGERIAL POSITION?

If you're considering making the move into management, it's important to understand the business side of therapy in addition to the treatment side. Show your supervisors that you have a desire to understand the function and growth of the clinic. Many of the decisions you will make as a manager will impact the business.

It is also important to understand the different departments in the clinic and the roles that they play. Ask to shadow different departments or take time to ask questions of colleagues in other departments.

HOW WILL I KNOW WHEN I'M READY TO TAKE ON MORE RESPONSIBILITY?

You might begin to feel stagnant as a treating therapist - like you've gotten all you can from where you are currently. You might want more of a challenge or something more dynamic to fill your days.

When you begin to feel that you aren't being challenged in your current role anymore, it's time to start considering what steps you might want to take to add responsibility and growth.

WHAT ADVICE DO YOU HAVE FOR SOMEONE INTERESTED IN LEADERSHIP OR MANAGERIAL POSITIONS?

STAY IN THE TRENCHES.

Don't remove yourself from treatment. By continuing to treat, you are able to keep yourself grounded. You are reminded how hard the work is and you will understand the amount of work the rest of the staff put in. If you keep a hand in the hard work, you will become a better leader. It's important to understand where the other therapists are coming from.

HOW DO I SHOW THAT I'M READY FOR A REHAB DIRECTOR POSITION IF I LACK LEADERSHIP EXPERIENCE?

EVERYBODY STARTS SOMEWHERE.
If a leadership role is your desired next step, be sure to let your employer know your goal. If your employer knows your career goal, they might more strongly consider you when opportunities for leadership surface internally.

There are also some steps you can start to take within your current role, such as performing additional tasks, in order to gain leadership experience. When you pick up extra tasks and gain leadership experiences, you can use them as talking points in interviews with future employers.

Be sure to update your resume as you grow. Perhaps within your resume, after performing some managerial tasks, you could change your job title to: PT Lead, Assistant Rehab Manager, etc. You can also include other non-work-related leadership experience on your resume, such as volunteer positions, military background, etc.

If you are ready for management position, you may want to apply to Director level positions. Even if a job advertisement says that a particular experience is required, there may be some situations where employers will look past the requirement and still consider you for the position.

The best Director level candidates are confident in their skills and communicate their desire to spread their wings in a leadership / managerial capacity.

Career Tree Network

HOW SHOULD I HANDLE MANAGING STAFF WHO HAVE BEEN THERE LONGER THAN I HAVE?

It can be tricky to manage therapists who were once your superiors. It's a balancing act to make them feel that they are able to voice their opinions and that you will take them seriously, but you ultimately have the final decision.

You can always invite their input and respect what they have to say, but at the end of the day you're the boss. It's not your job to befriend staff or make sure that everyone likes you; it's your job to make the best decisions for the clinic.

200 WORDS

LEAVING YOUR CURRENT JOB

ESSENTIAL CAREER ADVICE FOR THERAPY PROFESSIONALS

SHOULD I TELL MY CURRENT EMPLOYER THAT I'M CONSIDERING OTHER OPPORTUNITIES?

BEGIN WITH THE END IN MIND.
Before sharing with your current employer that you're exploring other opportunities, think about what you're hoping to gain by disclosing that to them.

If your end goal is to stay at your current employer but maybe renegotiate your current schedule or compensation, then you may want to tell your current employer that you're looking. That way, the two of you can ideally sit down and determine a path to continue your employment.

However, if your end goal is to leave and you know that it's time to move on...there's really no need to tell your employer that you're looking. If anything, it might make things awkward or you could potentially face termination.

When you have another position lined up, give your employer as much notice as you can; just because there's nothing more you want to accomplish doesn't mean you want to leave them in the lurch. (Two to four weeks notice is best.)

In summary...only confide in your employer if you're truly hoping there's a chance you can stay put. If you're 100% planning on leaving, then it's in your best interest to wait until you have another position lined up, give your notice, and move on.

HOW SHOULD I APPROACH MY CURRENT EMPLOYER ONCE I'VE SECURED A NEW POSITION?

No matter how great your relationship with your employer might be, telling them you're leaving can be awkward. You should approach the conversation directly and professionally, as you most likely want to keep a good relationship with them down the road.

Once you've got a job offer in hand, you'll want to verify the start date, so that you can give your employer as much information as possible. While two weeks notice is required for most organizations, giving your employer even more notice is the professional and respectful thing to do, if possible.

Don't beat around the bush. Give them as much notice as you're able to and be up front about your decision to move on. Thank them for the opportunity to work with them.

I'M FEELING BURNT OUT. HOW CAN I GET EXCITED ABOUT THERAPY AGAIN?

Burnout is commonplace in most fields of work. But as a therapy professional, you are especially prone to feeling the weight of your job. What you do is difficult and it's understandable that it would take a toll on you. But when you're feeling discouraged, do not despair! There are several things you can do to reignite your love of therapy.

One good way to deal with burnout is to pick up a PRN position within a different practice setting or a different organization. By mixing things up a little bit, you might start to feel excitement again. It's also great exposure to work with a different patient population than the patients you see from day to day.

Another option is to become a clinical instructor / mentor to a student or new grad. Typically they tend to have a lot of excitement for the field and the work they're doing. To work closely with them could benefit you by reminding you why you went into the therapy discipline!

Another, more extreme, option is to leave your position entirely. If you're feeling like you're dragging, perhaps a new practice setting can re-spark your excitement. Change is a good thing!

HOW DO YOU KNOW WHEN IT IS TIME TO RETIRE?

Before retiring, many therapists transition from full-time work to PRN in order to ease out of the field. It can be difficult to retire, because you no longer have the desire or necessity to work full-time, but you still love the profession. PRN provides a great opportunity to make a smooth transition.

When you reach a certain point in your career, you learn to listen to your mind and body, and allow them to be your guides in such decisions as retirement. If you have physical pain or you are not entirely mentally present, you are probably not providing your all for your patients. It may be time to scale back.

200 WORDS

ADVICE AND PERSPECTIVES FROM PRIVATE PRACTICE OWNERS

ESSENTIAL CAREER ADVICE FOR THERAPY PROFESSIONALS

WHY WOULD YOU DECIDE TO OPEN A PRIVATE PRACTICE?

If you reach a point in your career where you feel like you have learned everything you possibly can at your current job, you may consider opening a private practice.

Your strong reputation and loyal following from your current patients will follow you to your new practice.

Opening a practice can provide therapists with autonomy and freedom that restores or reinforces their love of the work.

WHAT ADVICE DO YOU HAVE FOR SOMEONE INTERESTED IN OWNING THEIR OWN PRACTICE?

If you're going to start a practice, don't do it straight out of school. Before you can become a great owner, you must first become a great clinician. Both are extremely important in opening a practice. Take a few years to become a good therapist, get a mentor, and really sharpen your skills.

You want to be sure that you can actually commit the time required to get your practice off the ground. It's a good idea to start small and build as the capital comes. The peace of mind you get from not over-committing is worth the gradual growth.

WHAT IS MOST ENJOYABLE ABOUT BEING A PRIVATE PRACTICE OWNER?

The most enjoyable part of being a private practice owner is the ability to run the clinic in the way that you believe therapy services should be provided. As an owner, you are constantly learning new things and are growing professionally.

You are always being stretched in new directions. There are a lot of ups and downs in running a business that some people don't enjoy, but many thrive on.

There is a freedom you experience as a Private Practice Owner that you just don't get in other roles. You spend your days working a job that you created for yourself; one that allows you to focus on your strengths and the things that give you joy.

WHAT IS LEAST ENJOYABLE ABOUT BEING A PRIVATE PRACTICE OWNER?

Sometimes, managing changes in staff is difficult and tiring. It can be challenging and extremely time consuming to find the perfect candidate for the job you have open.

Your business relies on great employees, and it is only as good as the team you choose. You must search for employees that share your values and reflect your vision for the clinic.

WHAT ARE THE GREATEST CHALLENGES THAT YOU FACE AS A PRIVATE PRACTICE OWNER?

The greatest challenges of owning a clinic are managing the payment models and competing with other providers.

In general, time management is difficult, but it is essential to the success of private practice owners. You never want to spread yourself too thin or over commit yourself, but it can be difficult when you feel like the success of the clinic rides on your shoulders.

WHAT IS SOMETHING THAT MOST PEOPLE DON'T REALIZE ABOUT OWNING A PRIVATE PRACTICE?

As a private practice owner, you work a lot! If you are a good clinician, it does not necessarily mean that you will be a successful practice owner. In order to succeed as an owner, you have to have grit, tenacity, and a strong drive.

While owning a clinic can be challenging, it is also quite rewarding.

Another thing that many people don't realize is that you don't make as much money as people think you do. You personally don't get paid what the clinic charges due to various overhead expenses. There are highs and lows, of course, but for many it's worth it.

Career Tree Network

IN THINKING ABOUT THE NEXT 10 YEARS, WHAT CHANGES DO YOU SEE COMING THAT MIGHT IMPACT PRIVATE PRACTICE OWNERS?

The future holds a continuing trend and transition toward value-based care. The practices that provide good care and good outcomes have to also provide good customer service.

The model of payment is also evolving, meaning that practices have to be cost effective.

There will also be more opportunities for therapists to do an increased amount of injury prevention down the road.

200 WORDS

THE BUSINESS SIDE OF HEALTHCARE AND THERAPY

ESSENTIAL CAREER ADVICE FOR THERAPY PROFESSIONALS

HOW CAN I PROVIDE GOOD CUSTOMER SERVICE?

To be successful in your career as a therapy professional, not only is it important to use proper techniques and treatment methods, it's also necessary to provide excellent customer service.

To start, involve patients in the treatment decision-making process. This approach empowers your patients and encourages them to take an active role in their healing process. It also creates trust between you and your patients. Also educate them on their treatment plan so they know what to expect.

Another way you can provide good customer service is through scheduling. Consider offering an online scheduling tool. It's easier for patients to make appointments and also convenient for you. In addition, schedule your time to include regular follow up calls to your patients to check on their progress. Your patients will appreciate your interest in their wellbeing.

Customer satisfaction surveys are essential in understanding where you can improve your service. Provide a survey at the end of each patient's care. Include questions regarding their visits, care and outcomes.

As always, great customer service includes a high level of professionalism. This means being courteous, friendly, on time, and an excellent communicator.

HOW CAN I DEAL WITH WORK RELATED STRESS?

Working as a therapy professional is rewarding, but can be stressful and emotionally draining. You're not alone. In 2012, 65 percent of Americans cited work as a top source of stress, according to the American Psychological Association's (APA) annual Stress in America Survey.

HERE ARE SOME WAYS TO COPE;
1. Make time for breaks. This includes lunch, one or two 15-minute breaks throughout your day, and taking your vacation time. This will help clear your head and help you come back to work refreshed.
2. Establish healthy boundaries between you and your patients. Maintaining a professional relationship will best serve you and your patients.
3. Learn how to relax. This may include breathing techniques and meditation.
4. Seek support from people you trust. Talk to loved ones, friends, a therapist, or your supervisor.
5. Keep active. When not at work, take time to do activities you love such as spending quality time with family and friends, taking on a fun project, or going to see a funny movie. These activities can boost your mood.

Always remember by taking care of yourself, you will be in a better position to help others.

Career Tree Network

WHAT ARE THE BEST STRATEGIES TO REPAY MY STUDENT LOANS?

On average, physical therapists have over $83,000 in student loans. Since most graduate and professional student loans accrue interest at a rate of 6.8%, the best practice is to make paying off student loans a priority. You have options.

You can search for a position that includes student loan repayment. These tend to be offered in rural / remote areas and may be worth looking into.

If you have federal loans, you may be eligible to defer these loans. For example, you qualify for deferment if you have not secured full-time employment. Consider reviewing the eligibility requirements for deferment to see if any apply to you.

If you are able, pay your federal loans according to the terms of your repayment plan. By remaining in good standing, you may qualify for the Public Service Loan Forgiveness (PSLF) Program in the future, which forgives the remaining balance on your federal loans.

Since interests rates fluctuate, you also have the option to refinance private loans for a better interest rate.

If you are overwhelmed with your loan repayments, there is a free service called FitBUX.com that offers tools and consulting to help customize your loan repayment plan based on your life goals.

WHAT DO I NEED TO KNOW ABOUT MARKETING?

Great marketing takes time, effort, and a well-thought out plan. It's also essential to grow your reputation. As a therapy professional, there are many aspects of marketing you will benefit from knowing. The first step is to create a marketing plan that will serve as a guide in your marketing efforts. The plan should include answers to the following questions:

- Who is your target market?
- Why should they choose your services?
- Where can they learn more about your services?
- What are your competitors doing and how can you stand out?
- What's going on in your industry and how are you staying on top of it?
- Which marketing tactics will you use to reach your market?
- How often will you market your services?
- What are your goals?
- What is your budget?
- What is your timeline?

Give careful thought and planning to your marketing tactics. It's important to leverage unique marketing avenues available to you to generate new patients. Once you have your plan in place, you will be off to the races.

SOME IDEAS ARE:
- Patient referral program
- Doctor referrals
- Partnerships with local organizations
- Sponsorships
- Ads in local publications
- Targeted social media ads

Career Tree Network

HOW DO I RECRUIT A THERAPY PROFESSIONAL TO JOIN MY TEAM?

There is an art and science behind effective recruitment strategies. Need to recruit a therapist to join your team? Remember to move quickly and sell first!

MOVE QUICKLY
The best candidates are hired quickly and are only available for a short period of time. With potential job offers from competing employers, recruiters will want to act with urgency to complete the hiring process. Aim to make contact with candidates within 24 hours. It is best if your initial contact is performed via both phone and email. (Text Message also works nicely for many candidates.)

SELL FIRST
Therapy professionals have a variety of career options. The ball is in their court and they hold the power. With that in mind, recruiters can not go out with guns blazing to grill candidates with fancy interview questions. For example, "Why do you want to join our team?" is an ineffective question for passive job seekers. Studies and observations found that to sell first and screen second works best. Thorough candidate screening is important, but that needs to happen after an effort is made to build candidate interest by sharing why the organization is a great place to work.

200 WORDS

THE FUTURE OF PHYSICAL THERAPY

ESSENTIAL CAREER ADVICE FOR THERAPY PROFESSIONALS

WHAT CHANGES HAVE YOU SEEN WITHIN THE PROFESSION?

One large change is the popularity and movement among therapists to go into private practice. The changes with insurance over the years have helped spur that movement.

For businesses, in the past, there was far less interdepartmental cooperation than there is today. Over the years, the relationships among PT, OT, SLP, and other departments have largely developed into holistic, respectful, and effective teams. This newer focus on interdepartmental teamwork is extremely beneficial to patients and to the work environment in general.

Treatment techniques have also changed in past years as more research has been funded and conducted.

WHAT ARE THE MOST EXCITING THINGS THAT THE FUTURE OF PHYSICAL THERAPY HOLDS?

There will definitely be an increasing involvement in the Home Health setting. This is an arena in which therapists are able to connect with their patients on a unique level, and provides the most comfortable services to patient as they are able to complete therapy from their homes.

The potential growth of physical therapy is also exciting. As awareness of the benefits of therapy increase, the field of work will continue to see an increase in patients.

WHAT IS MOST REWARDING ABOUT YOUR CAREER AS A THERAPY PROFESSIONAL?

One thing that is commonly overlooked as a rewarding piece of the therapy practice is the people to people relationships that you gain.

You have the ability to find great fulfillment in the relationships you form with patients. This profession exponentially grows your compassion if you allow it to.

The greatest satisfaction of your career may come from helping others see a brighter side of their future when things seemed at their darkest.

HOW OFTEN SHOULD I BE SETTING AND EVALUATING MY CAREER-RELATED GOALS?

Setting career goals is important...but goals are only effective if you commit to regularly evaluating them. When setting your initial career goals, start long-term and work your way down. Where do you see yourself in 10 years? What do you need to do in five years to get there? Two? One?

Once you've set your long and short-term goals, commit to checking in with them twice a year. Every six months, go over your career goals.

YOU CAN ASK YOURSELF CHECK-IN QUESTIONS LIKE THIS:
- Have I met a particular goal?
- Is it a realistic goal?
- Am I giving myself enough time to meet it, or does it need to be pushed back?
- Is it challenging enough?
- What am I doing each day to get myself closer to my goals?

Allow room for change, but make your goals concrete, measurable goals. That way, when you meet your goal, you won't have any question about whether or not you've reached it. You can cross it off, reevaluate, and move on to the next thing.

Career Tree Network

SPECIAL THANKS!

A huge thank you goes out to these people who provided their advice and knowledge of the field of therapy. We appreciate your experiences and stories. Without you, the creation of this book would not have been possible.

Amy Reiter
Amy Snyder
Annie Gerlach
Badieh Karps
Becky Thomas
Ben Solheim
Brett Roberts
Brianne Hemingway
Carmen Hilby
Connie Kittleson
Dorothy Purtell
Heidi Weidner
Janet Pointer
Jennifer Lavin
Jill Timm
Joanne Wirtz

Judith Exler
Kelly Ashbeck
Kelly Reeve
Kevin Svoboda
Kristin Lueptow
Leigha Slupski
Mark Erickson
Mary Dunne
Matthew Winney
Michelle Kastenholz
Nichole Ott
Rachel Hinterberg
Rob Worth
Susan La Croix
Tom Hughlett
Virginia Stoffel

Career Tree Network